SACRED PLACES

SACRED PLACES

Sarah Ann Osmen

St. Martin's Press, New York

A Sacred place of pilgrimage is a unique experiment.

It is a place where the currents are flowing from the places towards the soul, where the whole atmosphere is charged. From sacred places of pilgrimage, people have traveled to sublime heights, have become enlightened, and have seen visions of the divine. Such holy places have become charged areas due to centuries of events happenings there.

In such a place, if you do nothing else but throw open your sails, your journey will begin. This was the primary purpose and use for the sacred-place experiment.

Osho

SACRED PLACES
was produced by
Labyrinth Publishing S.A. Switzerland

Design by Sandipa Gould Griffin

Printed by Cronion S.A. Barcelona, Spain

Typeset on Apple Macintosh by Ma Premo (S. Castelli)
at Microprint – Via Pacini 49 / 51, Florence, Italy

Library of Congress Cataloging in Publication Data

Osmen, Sarah Ann
    Sacred Places / Sarah Ann Osmen
            p.   cm.
    ISBN 0 - 312 - 03513 - 6
    1. Sacred space.
    2. Sacred space -- pictorial works.
    I. Title
    [BL 580 • 075   1990]
    291 • 3' 5 -- dc 20
                                                89 - 78488
                                                   CIP

First Edition
10 9 8 7 6 5 4 3 2 1

CONTENTS

INTRODUCTION

THE HOLY AND THE HEARTH – SACRED POWERS – EARTH'S SACRED INDICATORS – KEYS TO THE HIDDEN MYSTERIES

Chapter 1 • p. 19

TEMPLES – THE SUPER SACRED

THE GREAT MYSTERY – THE COMMON TEMPLE - THE SECRETS OF EASTERN TEMPLES – THE SOUND OF SILENCE - FRAGRANCE AND LIGHT – THE ALCHEMY OF A SACRED PLACE – THE MAGICAL RADIUS – THE SACRED IMPRINT – THE SACRED ADORNMENT OF CAVE PAINTING – THE SHAMAN AS TEMPLE

Chapter 2 • p. 55

TEMPLES OF THE SUN AND MOON

CATCHING THE LIGHT – EARTH - MAN - EARTH – NEWGRANGE – THE POWER OF STONE – THE CONE OF SILENCE

Chapter 3 • p. 85

THE BIRTH OF EAST & WEST

THE CELTS – SACRED WATER, SACRED WOOD – THE CULT OF THE DRUIDS – THE EASTERN SIDE OF THE COIN

Chapter 4 • p. 103

THE HOLY LANDS

THE COMING OF CONFLICT – STEPS IN THE HOLY LAND – THE BEGINNINGS OF THE HOLY LAND – JERUSALEM THE ETERNAL – JERICHO – INDIA – HOLY MOUNTAIN OF THE JAINS – THE CITY OF LIGHT – MAYA – THE PERUVIAN HUMMINGBIRD

Chapter 5 • p. 127

THE ROMAN MIGHT

RELIGIOUS ORDER – THE ROMAN MYSTERIES – THE CULT OF MITHRA – SEVEN STEPS TO HEAVEN – EGYPT, GREECE AND THE GODS OF NATURE

Chapter 6 • p. 143

HOLY WELLS, WATERCOURSES & THE LEY

WATER EVERYWHERE – LEADING TO THE LEY – LEY-VISIONS THE TALES OF DE-COO-DAH

Chapter 7 • p. 171

THE CHRISTIAN BEGINNING

A NEW CULT – VIKINGS, MASTERS OF THE PAGAN PAST – THE RUNES OF A SACRED ALPHABET – THE CHRISTIAN CULT – MARY, MOTHER OF GOD – THE RISE AND FALL OF WICCA

Chapter 8 • p. 183

CRYPTIC KARMA

CRYSTALLIZING THE ANCIENTS – THE ENIGMA OF ENLIGHTENMENT – GROUNDS FOR BELIEF – THE OSHO ASHRAM – THE SACRED SEDIMENT OF MEDITATION – THE SACRED BODY

Chapter 9 • p. 199

THE SILENT TEMPLE

THE ALONE – MYSTIC AND MEANING

Chapter 10 • p. 209

THE ANCIENT MEASURERS

THE MAGIC ONE – MEASURING THE PYRAMID OF CHEOPS

Chapter 11 • p. 219

THIS SACRED PLACE

SO ANCIENT, SO FOREIGN, SO NEW

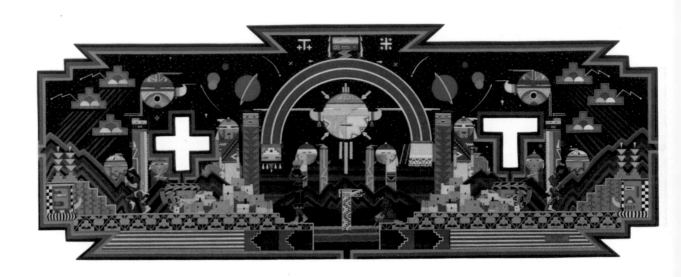

Introduction

THE HOLY
& THE HEARTH

Hundreds of thousands of sacred locations dot the surface of this planet like a memory system of the most ancient and sacrosanct past.

In every country there are sacred monuments of the oldest religious traces of mankind. From the oldest stone circles in the UK, the American Indian's "ley" line monuments, the astonishing Mexican temples to the Celtic arbors of the sacrificial rituals of the Druidic priests sacred monuments remind us that we have a source, a real source purer and more powerful than any of the modern problems of life can wipe out.

SACRED PLACES is a book about why we create sacred places and from whom we have learned to build them – from our ancestors, from our Gods and from our natural connection with life

Mankind cannot live without the holy, even in his everyday life and in his home he has almost invariably a sacred element – "Home is where the heart is" – and where the heart is, so there is religiousness in its broadest sense. But our older and more established sacred places are very often a mystery to us. What do the stories of places such as Newgrange signify? Why are so many parts of the world covered in ancient tracks and "ley" lines? What were our ancient ancestors intending when they built their monuments upon these tracks?

Why were "bluestones" transported hundreds of miles across Wales and England to build the early Stonehenge and what are the hints which may have been laid down by distant ancestors to tell us why they put it there? Where did the Celts come from and what is their intimate connection with the Hindus on the other side of the world? The answers to these questions may be keys to our modern need to feel the presence of sacrosanct earth for we are once again returning to an interest in the "true religion," disillusioned perhaps by the organized Churches.

Sacredness on Earth is a little like a computerized memory bank. It is as though the past races of mankind wanted to leave certain essences and stories for the future and did so by laying tracks upon the earth that give us magic and mystery. We interpret these messages, according to our own present-day experience when we should be looking deeper into the center of man in order to find the answers.

What comes to mind when we consider the word "sacred"? Perhaps we associate it with religion, with places of worship – churches, burial grounds, ancient tombs. These places probably originally earned the title sacred because of their associations with the mystical and mysterious, something even other-worldly; and today, although the strength of the original power of organized religion may have diminished, there is still potentially the same strength remaining of the ancient feeling of sacredness. Sacred places are also nearly always old places so that the concept of sacredness is also tied in with having been around for a long time. But age is not the only qualification of holy ground, otherwise cities such as Florence or Athens or even parts of London would be sacrosanct – there are plenty of old places that are clearly not sacred!

These sacred monuments and markings take all manner of forms, not simply cathedral-like constructions such as we have built during "recent" centuries, but places such as the standing stones of Callanish seen on this page or the astonishing Ridge of Nazca opposite. Standing stones may perhaps have had a variety of purposes – not only the astronomical observance of the seasonal changes but also curative purposes for all manner of physical ailments. Edicts passed in Europe between A.D. 450 and 1100 illustrate this fact, prohibiting the use of stones for the cure of sickness. This period was the very beginning of the spread of Christian doctrine, in which Church and authority banded together to attempt to prevent the pagan ways of the people.

The Ridge of the mountainous hill at Nazca in Peru, shown opposite, is perhaps one of the world's strangest sacred places. The top of the hill has been sheared off to make an elongated platform several miles long with triangles and intricate designs and markings on the left of the "runway". There have been many suggestions as to what this may have been for, such as a landing strip for flying saucers flown by extra-terrestrial beings, for the precise measurement of the strip would have required very advanced techniques and equipment, perhaps in advance of those available at the time of its completion.

SACRED POWERS

Sacredness in fact is something very tangible. If we look a little more closely at structures such as the Kali Temple in Calcutta, an obviously sacred place, we find some very clear and tactile aspects – smells, shapes, the materials employed in the architecture – that have somehow increased in power over the centuries and which seem to maintain the mystery and impact of a building which is unique in its appeal to human nature. By comparison with "normal" structures such as the Empire State Building or the Eiffel Tower, for example, Calcutta's Kali Temple stands out as different in a very obvious way. Walking into the Empire State Building in New York inspires a certain awe, but that feeling is associated with the size of the place rather than anything else. There is nothing that touches the soul of the explorer, for the atmosphere is not something which reaches down inside us. Most of us have visited

The ancient temples of India such as the one opposite, are perhaps more grand and elaborate than any in the world. The Hindus, grown from the "Battle-Axe" people who split into two of the religious foundations of this planet – the Celts and the Hindus – traveled across Persia and India to erect their extraordinary temples to the Hindu God. The Celts, on the other hand, blonde instead of dark, tall instead of short and powerful warriors instead of peaceful people, created few standing monuments, worshipping their God, the Mother Earth, the Moon and the trees and animals. There could perhaps have been no two races more different grown from a single source.

By contrast to the temples of India in all their golden glory, there stands Venice, on the opposite page, a tribute to the Western world that in a great part grew out of the Celtic tribes. This picture from the artist Ippolito Caffi and named "Venezia sotto la neve".

at least one sacred place in our lives: it might only be a particular church that seems special in a way we cannot define – perhaps there is a sense of meditation, of peace that makes us feel silent and still, or perhaps the constant smell of incense creates an atmosphere of mystery that changes our otherwise worldly feelings. It is often as though we can find a special kind of energy inside such buildings that gives us something we cannot find elsewhere and many people still enter their local churches simply to enjoy that particular sense of calm.

The theme of this book, then, is to explore the common features that occupy the sacred places of the world, their qualifications for our label "sacred," and to look inside some of the most fascinating sacred places and see what it is that has caused us to be attracted to them and why we felt the need to create them in the first place.

In past centuries mankind has injected the most astonishing amounts of energy into erecting structures such as the Duomo in Florence, a cathedral that took no less than three hundred years to build: five or six generations of the best architects, planners, builders and masons to erect one enormous stone building in the name of the Christian God. Such structures began their lives as simple pieces of stone. There was a time when the ground that is now occupied by the Duomo was simply covered in grass or dirt. Its surface was in no way hallowed or special. People walked across it without any sense of awe or dignity. Even once the foundations of the building had been laid, huge blocks of stone which were then overlaid with marble, still there was no particular sense of anything Godly for the materials were simply hewn from rock and fashioned into square shapes for the purpose of creating something which would eventually be called a cathedral.

Over the centuries that it took to finish this extraordinary work of architecture, the people perhaps began to feel a certain

excitement as they watched gifted masons chipping away at rough marble, creating the shapes of the heavenly host. Perhaps those that stood looking at these transformations began to feel the first sensations of sacredness and those that created them injected some kind of energy into the stone which increased its power over mankind's emotions. As the vaulted arches and buttresses reached higher and higher towards the heaven that people of the time worshiped, so the sense of awe and excitement evoked by the cathedral grew stronger and once the work was completed, those that had begun it centuries earlier were long dead and their sons'

The Duomo – for those who have lived in Florence, like the author, this extraordinary temple to man's religious passion grows like a wondrous and splendid love affair. In many ways it seems not to matter to which God it was erected for it dominates both the senses and the beliefs of all who see it. More than three centuries in the building, architects, stone masons and builders passed on from generation to generation the task of creating this astonishing monument.

The Duomo is perhaps one of the most extravagant examples of what the Christian Church brought to mankind – its power and grace of immense significance – but perhaps we can also briefly examine the other side of the religious coin insofar as the force with which the Christian Church subdued the religious beliefs that it followed.

Our attitude toward Earth was healthier when we were pagans who believed that spirits resided in everything, that man and beast were on equal footing, and trees had to be placated before cutting. – Kenneth Brower.

The sheer size and substance of a monument such as the Duomo not only exemplifies the strength of the Church that it represents, but also the extent of the suppression that this same Church exacted upon the ancient pagan rites of the people. These people in their hundreds of generations had worshipped something far more powerful than a massive bulk of stone and cement – they worshiped the Earth itself and everything that naturally grew upon it. Their concept of religion was based upon a very personal appreciation of life, nature and a wholeness which we have now largely lost. The very idea of suppressing any of the human involvements in life such as love, sexuality, relationships with God or humanity was beyond their understanding and only became prevalent once the Church authorities began to insist upon a particular kind of God – a wrathful, exacting God who demanded that mankind live according to His rules. This demanding behavior seems to have been largely responsible for all the misery, war and distress that mankind has forced himself to deal with in the two thousand years of organized religion.

sons and daughters had given birth through many families before finally, those who stood and looked up at the spires and domes were able to sample the beginning of sacred worship. From then on, the combined and individual energy injected into such buildings has continued to create more and more special feelings surrounding the original simple stone. The religious ceremonies, the singing of hymns, the gathering of "like minds" has continued to pour a certain expression into the ancient cathedrals and holy gathering places of the world: like huge cups filled with human energy, such places are now filled with our past.

EARTH'S SACRED INDICATORS

Imagine an alien visitor coming to this planet, perhaps bringing some energy "detector" to figure out how we operate. This detector might be tuned to a certain level in order to find out which buildings have accumulated the maximum amount of complex and deep-set power generated by the attention of the human race. Which would be the sacred places that would register on this "holy energy detector"? Would it zone in on the Taj Mahal or Coventry Cathedral? Would it perhaps find its way to discover the built-up energy in the depths of the many Indian temples of worship, the ancient Eastern ashrams or Stonehenge, Avebury and

The Easter Island figures, their bases buried deeper in the ground even than their heads stand above it, were placed at angles that allow them a direct view of the moon. The pagan beliefs that created the determination to erect such monuments was deeply concerned with the moon's power to change the seasons and influences of Earth's climate and life, yet another example of man's concern for his planet.

Newgrange? Would the spots of sacredness scattered across the globe standing out on the gauge include such places as the Temples of Java, the Giant's Apron and the Devil's Spade in Britain, Chartres and other great ancient cathedrals, the Sphinx, the Egyptian Pyramids, the Bermuda Triangle, the Easter Island stone heads? And would such visitors find links between these incredible places which might suggest to them that mystical powers that existed in ancient times specifically laid down messages for the future through such sacred places? Perhaps there are hidden truths still lingering within our heritage of holy ground that will one day reveal these secrets to us.

J.Krishnamurti said that it needed only a hundred people meditating together at one time for the energy of the planet to be changed for the better. Groups of modern religious disciples have begun to gather together during this century to a greater extent than for many hundreds of years, perhaps because we need this influence more than ever before. The effects of such energy are seen to be wide-spread in their power with cosmic implications that return to the planet after circling the universe. Sacred places, then, may even be created by the temporary gathering together of meditators.

Keys to the Hidden Mysteries

Suppose we had an old, rusty key that had been in our possession all our lives. The preciousness of an old key might lie in its power to unlock a door to some great and precious treasure from the past. But alas, we don't know where the treasure is, nor where the lock we might be able to open is, and thus the key is useless. In fact, it's not even a key at all, because it cannot open any lock. It becomes in this case just a piece of rusty iron.

Even if we broke it into pieces it would not reveal to us the way to the hidden treasure. However, we cannot work up enough courage to throw it away; in a remote corner of our hearts we hope that some day some lock might be found that it fits.

Such keys are to be found scattered all over the world, wherever man has lived. Temples, pyramids, standing stones, ground markings, mysteries for which we have no explanation and which seem to have been present since time immemorial. We suspect that these sacred places are representations of a great knowledge which is now lost, left to us as a heritage, just like an old key. We do not know how to unlock their secret doors, but we cannot destroy them because a sixth sense tells us that they mark a path, a wisdom which we may have inherited.

The book that follows, then, examines such places and many more, in an attempt to find out the central and likely features of the most important sacred places on earth in the hope that perhaps there are linking factors within these structures which we have long lost sight of – mystical and mysterious truths which, once revealed, will take us into a completely new way of looking at them.

Without wishing to become involved in
too much enigma, we might just become
aware that there are more things in
heaven and earth than we know of!
Sacredness contains elements of
"complete" mystery – i.e. that which we
can *never* know. We can even say that the
moment we know, the mystery is gone.

TEMPLES
THE SUPER SACRED

THE GREAT MYSTERY

One of the great tragedies of modern Western religious conditioning is that it has almost totally lost touch with the myths of mankind. Organized religion today relies only on its history, on events and personalities such as those related in the Bible, or the Koran, which cast aside the so-called pagan stories and rituals of the more distant past.

One of the major results of this denial, for the majority of people today, is a fundamental misunderstanding of sacredness. The great "mystery" of the ancient past was purely a matter of accepting the mystery of the universe and feeling its power through the presence of all sensual objects. Mankind could see with his eyes, hear, touch, smell, taste, all objects within his surroundings, but these were merely pointers to the "rest," fingers indicating the presence of the divine, so that mystery was that which he could not sense with those certain organisms in his possession, but it was also that which he worshipped in the broadest possible sense of the word – it was his religiousness. As such, then, everything in his environment was sacred because everything pointed towards divinity.

The modern Masters – those that bemuse us, confuse us and sometimes irritate us with their uniqueness – men and women

Everything points towards the divine. The magic of this understanding, once absorbed, is that it permeates that same "everything" that we have so long been denying. A simple acceptance of *all* life rather than one or other part of it gives a totally new conception to each act that we perform. Here lies sacredness.

The ancient Chinese, thousands of years ago, well appreciated many of the "scientific" and spiritual aspects of life which we are today only just waking up to again. To appreciate and absorb the bamboo the adept had to "become" the bamboo – get inside it, so to speak. This required stillness and a denial of worldly preoccupations, even if only for an hour each day. We have not lost this ability but simply forgotten it.

Many men and women have touched upon a divinity which promises a higher sacredness throughout the ages. On this page are but a few of them –

Gurdjieff, Ramana Maharshi, The Mother, Krishnamurti, Ramakrishna, Meher Baba,

The Celtic swordsmen and women – warriors and priests – combined an extraordinary belief in the sanctity of nature alongside gruesome sacrificial rituals. Their beliefs perhaps give modern man a sense of horror and revulsion for there was much blood upon the trees of their sacred arbors. But the issue central to Celtic beliefs was that man was as much an element of earth's wholeness as were the plants, the seasons and the trees so that to kill a man or woman was simply an act suitable to encourage the continued seasonal fullness of the earth and therefore of the harvest. They would bury the body of the sacrificed human in the land that would swallow his blood and thus bring better crops the next year. The extravagance of the simple flower represented as great a power as the drama of the human body.

mostly from the East, tell us this same story, perhaps in a slightly different way. They point at everything around us and tell us that each and every aspect of life is divine, sacred. Even the finest blade of grass contains the essence of the sacrosanct.

Our tragedy in the West is that we have somehow "raised" our level of consciousness, not in a spiritual sense but in a physical sense, to levels that concentrate for their satisfaction on the degree of sensory reward through results. We adore the motor vehicle, the house, the bank account and all the numerous possessions that are available through the consumer social structure, and in so doing we lose our more sensitive appreciation of the divinity of simplicity. Who looks at a tree or a flower, a bird or a small insect and feels the sense of divinity that these smaller items of life can transmit?! And yet it is these things, tiny and almost immediately forgettable, that comprise the real essence of sacred appreciation.

Perhaps because mankind was aware of his own ability to ignore nature, he set down larger "temples" for the appreciation of divinity. Perhaps because he knew that he was soon to become

too busy for the enjoyment of simple perfection, he decided to
build or create edifices of a more obvious and substantial power
that might remind him of the original, pagan beliefs and adorations
of the ancient past. The temples built were, in effect, unavoidable
pointers to divinity, planned to give a very simple message: enter
here and find God, not the God that we appraise as our Father and
"leader," in the modern organized religious sense, but a God that
completely surrounds us and exists in all things – if we like, a
pantheistic God.

THE COMMON TEMPLE

There is no race in Earth's history which has not erected or created temples. Whether they are called mosques, churches or gurudwaras is not important – the temple is common to all civilizations. The modern science of archaeology has revealed in the last two centuries that some of the temples were built thousands of years ago, at a time when there was no link between the races of this planet. Therefore, the temple is not an imitation from other civilizations, but is the result of a completely spontaneous process of human consciousness. Anywhere there is a human settlement, whether it is in remote corners, in places of utter solitude, on hills, mountains, by the side of lakes and rivers, on vast planes or within the dark meanders of tropical forests, man has always built temples. Outwardly there is a great difference between a Christian church, a Moslem mosque, a Hindu place of worship or even a pre-historic shamanic cave, but as far as the aspiration and the inner surge is concerned there is no difference.

The keys to some of these temples, why they came into being and what our ancestors did within their walls, have been lost to us. There is very little knowledge that might enlighten us – to modern man they are rudiments of a past which he cannot understand. There are things in our lives that persist despite all attempts to destroy them. Our sense of the divine is probably one of the strongest of survivors, thus our persistent creation of edifices to the numerous Gods that have lived alongside us.

We may satisfactorily state that one of the differences between

The Burmese temple across these two pages is the U Min Kyaokse Pagoda in Sagaing. Temples have been a feature of man's belief in divinity from long before the different races of humanity were aware of one another so that a common understanding of divine worship existed in many different parts of the planet independent of one another. The original beliefs have been seen to survive all attempts to suppress them as though we are fundamentally the same regardless of our civilizing changes, constantly returning to the same inner appreciation of religiousness.

man and beast is that man erects temples and beast does not. Every creature provides shelter for itself, but to build edifices and shrines for God seems to be a prerogative of man. No such edifice could be built without a deep experience of the divine; even if that experience were later to be lost, the temple would still continue to stand to remind us of it.

Suppose we were to build a guest house attached to or nearby our home: the fact that we are prepared to spend money and energy on such an enterprise proves that guests have been coming. The whole idea of building temples and shrines must have been conceived in such moments when God was a living reality for men, a reality confirmed by the experience of many people and not based solely on the eccentric fancy of someone's imagination.

Let us use a simple analogy to see in which way our ancestors

On the following pages we take a pictorial look at the temples of the Far East, structures that vary in their architecture, their grandeur and their focus but nevertheless remain the same in the basis of their appreciation of divinity. The Mayan, Chinese, Thailand, Russian and Christian edifices, lined across the following spread in that order, show us the variations that spread across almost the entire world from east to west.
One of the most landlocked spots in Asia lies deep in the Chinese province of Sinkiang, a mountain-circled wilderness with a heart of desert. The Himalayas lay to the south – the mountains still today rising at the rate of six inches each year depriving the whole area of the monsoon rains and the desert heat also evaporating all but one of the rivers fed by the melting snows before they ever reach any sea. This was the area where the famous and ancient Silk Road began, running from old Mongolia for five thousand miles to Venice, traveled by Marco Polo and the communication for the first traders between east and west, from the seat of the violent and powerful kingdoms of the Khans to the civilization of merchants of Europe. The mighty forests that stood along the way have literally deteriorated and died during the historical memory of this short period.

ensured receptivity and manifestation of God. Imagine that there is a great war and technology, as we know it today, is lost. A radio escapes destruction and survives in your household. Even though you may not be able to receive any broadcast through the radio, you might want to keep it as a memento to be passed from your generation to the next. Your descendants will not understand its utility because they have never used the instrument and it will be very difficult for them to understand that it used to act as a receiving station for something happening elsewhere and that it used to catch waves and present them as sounds to the listeners.

We find ourselves in the same position as those puzzled

The picture on this page right illustrates just one of the Great Wall of China's fortresses – the Jiayuguan Fort – the very last on the wall itself. The Great Wall represented China's hatred of nomadic tribal wanderings, their determination to ground themselves amidst the awesome wilderness of the China deserts – to bring order and harmony to The Celestial Kingdom ruled by The Son of Heaven. Beyond the wall lay darkness. Still today, the Chinese who inhabit the area speak of those who go past the wall as beyond the pale – going "outside the mouth".

And across the center of this spread stands one of the dramatic Thailand temples, held in place by a single warrior, the levels of the architecture like steps into the sky.

Russian mosques, Christian cathedrals, Mayan temples – all tell the same story of man's passion for his various Gods and the desire to reach higher into oblivion.

descendants would be, were such a thing ever to happen. In exactly the same way as a radio, temples used to function as receptive instruments for the omnipresence of God. Though we can say that God is everywhere and man is also everywhere, only by some specific adjustment within us can some sort of communication become possible between us and God. The arrangements within a temple were such that they would enable men and women to feel the divine existence and spiritual elevation by which their personality might open up to and receive divinity. Such may have been the motivations behind the elevation of temples and shrines.

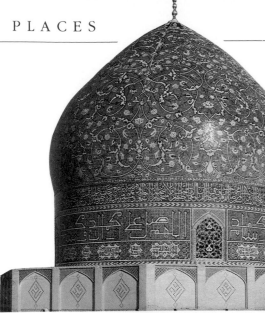

The Secrets of Eastern Temples

India is perhaps the richest country in the world in terms of tradition, a country where roots can be traced back for thousands of years. Here some of the most intriguing sacred places are to be found.

Indian temples were built according to three or four patterns and the model of the sky was copied in their construction. There was a specific purpose behind the semi-circular shape of the domes that roofed the abode of Indian Gods. When somebody chants AUM, mantra chanting being one of the main forms of prayer in Eastern tradition, the dome of the temple echoes the sound, sending it back, thus forming a circle. Although the sound produced is human, when it is echoed back it resounds with a new speed and other potentialities are released as it is re-imbibed. When we sit alone, practicing this sound-prayer, and the circle formation is set, then we may well feel as though our prayers have been answered! With the resonance, the divine experience begins to enter the worshiper. Outwardly a circle of sound is formed, inwardly all thought comes to an end and the worshiper might simply sit there forever like the Buddha statues we see sitting in padmasan or siddhasan.

But one of the single features that separates the temples across the previous two pages and the one from which the illustration is taken opposite, is the presence of erotic sculpture.

It is rarely if ever that we see any kind of sexual display on either Far Eastern temples or those of Russia or Europe, whereas in India the sight of orgiastic activities is quite common amongst the Hindi Tantric temples of the East.

The Tantric adept was concerned to reach his particular nirvana through sexual union with a woman and with death. The two taboos were intimately linked – life and death were one.

Disciples lived and still do live near to burial grounds and their total concern is with the "yoni" of the female provider, from which and into which all spiritual growth derives.

The chakras of the body and the study of the human levels of physical energy derive from the Hindu Tantric beliefs and these extraordinary temples in the highly repressed surroundings of Indian life reflect this belief.

The Sound of Silence

One of the main features of the Indian temple was acoustics, the sound produced by voices, bells, gongs, reflected back from the roof or walls of the inner temple. Sound always moves in reflection and certain sounds have certain effects, some damaging and some curative.

The Sufi followers direct their entire search for divinity through music – the music of the universe, which brings balance and forms a law hidden behind all aspects of life, holding the universe intact and fulfilling its purpose.

Many of the modern masters of divinity have also compared music with silence – that music is the next thing to silence, separated only by the air's breadth. *Many say that life entered the human body by the help of music, but the truth is that life itself is music.* Hafiz.

In the temples of India then, sound is considered to be of the greatest importance and even though often the western visitor may be shocked by the small windowed, strange-smelling temples that he encounters, the monks are healthy and strong and maintain that it is the sound of *AUM* reflected off the walls and ceilings that keep them this way.

At the entrance of Indian temples we also find bells or gongs which have exactly the same purpose. The sound they produce reminds the visitor of the mantra AUM and of the circle of sound.

The acoustics and the architecture of a temple have a deep significance and their effects on the human body may go beyond all present expectations. When Westerners first visited Indian temples they declared them unhygienic places since there were no windows and only the smallest of entrances. They were dark places and the monks that practiced these meditations lived in poor huts nearby. It all appeared dirty and primitive to a mind accustomed to the big spaces of the Christian cathedrals. However, thousands of years of such practices had not led the monks to ill health; on the contrary, they were the healthiest people in the country. First of all no disease was ever allowed within holy precincts. And what is most fascinating of all, is that the chanting of the sound AUM and the sound circle which is formed within the walls of the meditation chamber has a unique purifying effect. Ancient sages believed that sound was an altered form of electricity and that special sounds can cause special effects.

It has now been proved by Western scientists that sound has beneficial effects on small babies, on birthing methods, on plant cultivation and all sorts of areas that affect the environment directly and subtly. For Indian mystics the temples were experimental laboratories and the science of acoustics, which has now been almost totally lost, was held in great consideration for it was used experimentally on the human body. Ancient treatises stipulate rules stating from what angles to direct the sounds at the body – what sound should be made in the sitting posture and which sound is appropriate for the standing posture. Which sounds should be made together and which separately. Indian musical compositions and dances were first developed in the temples and later on they developed elsewhere as specific arts.

The Vedic scriptures were also based on the same principle of

And with sound comes of course dance. The two are almost indivisible for movement derives from music and music from movement.
The ancient tribes used both music and dance for their rituals, for the encouragement of the season's gifts to their crops and for the festivities that accompanied fertility rites. The picture on this page depicting dancers is drawn from the men of the Hapaee tribe in the South Pacific during a night ritual for the coming seasonal celebrations and the strength of the tribe.

sound forming an electrical circle: the emphasis of the scriptures was phonetic rather than linguistic and the wisdom contained therein was passed from generation to generation by word of mouth. When the scriptures were translated from the original Sanskrit language into Western tongues, thus emphasizing the linguistic aspect, the wisdom of the scriptures was completely lost and in fact there are passages which could not be understood because they did not make any sense from a linguistic standpoint. For instance, the meaning of the Tibetan mantra OM MANI PADME HUM is impossible to explain, because its significance lies totally in its phonetics.

And sound was not the only aspect of the diagnosis for sacredness. There was also the presence of fragrance and of light.

Containing the celestial movements of a planet around its own axis and then around the sun, the Dervish, in his whirling meditations, realizes the spiraling of the universe. They say that the spirit reduces to matter at the center of his axis, at his heart, as he spins. His right hand receives the manifestation of the One, and his left hand earths the spirit received. With the whirling, the meditator loses the complexities of the mind, for there is no space for confusion, only centering and perfecting. For those who have only once tried it and found the method, there can never be another way. These Dervish dancers are of the order of Mevlevi from Konya in Turkey.

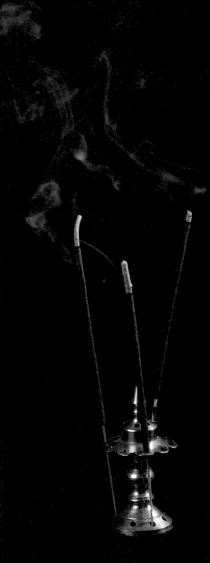

Fragrance and Light

In entering an active Indian temple, one of the first things that can shock the visitor is the hazy, smoky atmosphere within, and the intense, suffocating smell of burning incense. Bewildering as it may seem, the smells exuded from different types of burning incense are deeply connected with the science of sound vibration, and this combination of sound and fragrance is what creates an atmosphere of holiness within a sacred place.

Certain fragrances blend harmoniously with certain sounds, because the vibrations produced by those particular sounds also emanate, believe it or not, particular fragrances.

The incense from lobhan is used in Moslem mosques. One of the forms of Moslem prayer is the chanting of Allah-Hoo repetitively. Stress is put on the Hoo and after a while Allah will naturally disappear and only the Hoo can be heard in the continuous chanting. If this form of sound is chanted for long enough, it is said that the smell of lobhan will emanate from the body of the adept.

Different religious practices use different burning incense for this reason and the modern, popular science of aromatherapy can give us some practical examples which we can experience by simply sitting in a room.

Light has been, for centuries, the most central of sacred elements. From the very earliest monuments such as Newgrange where the light of sun and moon were employed to indicate the seasonal changes, up to the cathedral stained glass window where light is employed to enlighten the saints and the holy. This illustration is of the Rose window at the West Front of Chartres Cathedral created between 1197 and 1260.

Between lovers, smell is also important – we will not wish to kiss a man or woman whose smell does not agree with us. On the other hand, we will enjoy the smell of our personal partner and miss it when it is absent. We may say that the energy of the partner is vibrating at a speed that is congenial to us, and the smell of his or her body is emanating as a manifestation of that harmony.

Sandalwood paste became very popular in Eastern temples and the place on the forehead where sandalwood is applied is called the ajna chakra in yoga. By chanting certain mantras the body produces a sandalwood fragrance and when the paste is applied on the forehead it gives a soothing, balming feeling to the whole body and one can recall the same experience as when chanting those mantras.

The presence of fragrance is therefore seen as a vital part of the sacredness of a building. The smells that have been formed within the sacred place over hundreds of years help to build the holy atmosphere and retain its communication with God. The concepts of God and religiousness are seen, in this light, as eternal presences – atmospheres, rather than outside entities.

We can see this, very simply, in our own homes. The constant presence of the human fragrances, of people, of flowers, of incense, all contribute to the sacred nature of that home. When we leave a house to move elsewhere, we will often remember the fragrances that remain as part of our lives. Just the same essences are retained within the more traditional holy temples of the East and West.

Light is also of the utmost importance in aiding and altering the psyche. We know this well from the lighting we choose for our homes. In temples certain lighting techniques are carefully used: in Indian temples "ghee" burning lamps are used, ghee being a fatty substance derived from butter without the cream. In Catholic churches we find dark interiors lit by a profusion of candles, which are sometimes scented with pure incense.

Finally, the essences that make up the sacred environment are transformed by the ancient art of alchemy.

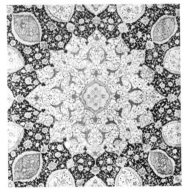

Smell and light even pervade the relationships that we encounter in life – a chemical balance being needed for people to be attracted to one another.

The mandala, as a reflection of the universe in mathematical and design aspects. The above Sufi mandala combines mysticism and precision. This illustration taken from *Chahar taq* near Kashan, Iran and forming the center of the Ardabil carpet made in 1540.

THE ALCHEMY OF A SACRED PLACE

Rembrandt's portrait of Dr Faustus in his study gives us the essence of the alchemist.

Alchemy is seen today only as an empty and probably useless ritual – the attempts of the ignorant to make gold from base metal. But the practice of alchemy was far more than this and it is we who are the ignorant for our determination to base everything upon the so-called precision of science. The alchemical processes were never intended to act with prejudice as does modern science. There was never seen to be any purpose in naming a substance and then defining it. The alchemist was a magician in the widest sense of the word – his intention being to transform the mysteries while still maintain their mystical values. He did not wish to label life but only to understand it and accept it.

Alchemy is an old science which has traveled the path hand in hand with the awareness that human consciousness is susceptible to the five elements. All religious traditions have practices based on alchemical principles which are now forgotten and performed only as rituals, largely empty of meaning. Sacred places were born out of alchemical experiments and our understanding of the basic principles is essential to unlock the doors to spiritual and human understanding.

Each sacred place, temple or physical site has its own exact science; one step follows another until the end of the process and if one step is missed on the way then the path may be lost even to the most devoted of adepts. Signs and keys have been left by those who reached the path before us, in order to help us follow. For example, in Buddhist Tibetan and Hindu tradition, a special piece of metal alloy with figurines carved on the surface is used to this purpose. Similar "keys" may also be found hanging on household walls with the words "prosperity and goodness" inscribed under or around them. The true purpose of such "keys" is to impress a figure onto the consciousness of the user. In just the same way, if we stare at a window frame for five minutes without blinking, upon closing the eyes the "imprint" of the window frame is still there. By seeing the key again and again the adept may impress the image and be able to recall it when it is needed along the spiritual path. Without knowing their purpose, rituals and customs may seem utterly futile to us, but even a superficial grasp of the alchemical principle may help to bring back to life many of the traditions which still exist today.

By performing an action involving one of the five elements, repeatedly, perhaps even for the whole of one's life, consciousness is altered and so is the chemistry of the element. The alteration caused by a particular repetitive action is designed to bring the performer to the full flowering of his self.

Hindu scriptures, for instance, emphasize that the yogi should consume enough milk, curd and ghee to maintain a balanced amount of moisture in his body. All Hindu sacred places are set along the banks of the river Ganges and bathing in the river is one of the holiest forms of ritual. Hindu religion is centered around the element of water in this way. The Hindus also send their dead down the Ganges as part of the religious tradition. Dead bodies have been floating in the Ganges for thousands of years and still the water is not foul-smelling. In effect this religious tradition is an alchemical experiment in the return of the human body to its original holy temple within the river.

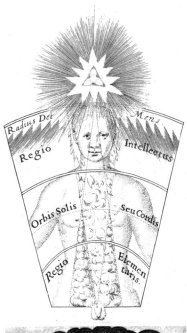

The ultimate alchemy is, of course, the alchemical changes of life – the birth, physiology, psychology, death and transformation of the human being. The elements take a shape and form and then go back to earth once more and the story begins again in a different form. All alchemy in effect reflects this cycle.

The Magical Radius

A sacred place can be defined as such because it emanates an influence which goes beyond its physical form. It influences the psyche of man, his surroundings and sometimes even his nature, as well as animals. Temples provide an aura of purity and peace.

Teilhard de Chardin has coined the word "noosphere" to describe a particular mental and psychological outlook, a "field" surrounding a place or a person.

It was once the tradition of Tibetan monasteries that if something undesirable happened within the grounds of the temple the master would himself suffer the penance rather than administer punishment to his disciples. The very committing of that act meant

The magic circle permeates all life and today even transforms our awareness of it through science. Rupert Sheldrake, a British biologist has proposed the existence of morphological fields, movements of continuously changing energy that surround us all in everything we do. Like auras of energy these fields are habits of existence and map all actions. The oldest stories repeat in new forms.

that the field that surrounded the holy place had lost its quality, and that punishing the monks would have been therefore pointless. The master of the monastery took it upon himself to seclude in meditation with fasts and self-purification in order to redress the balance of the field.

Temples can be a very powerful influence on the external world, as if they were meant to be a sort of experiment on the external level. There is still today much suspicion surrounding temples and churches, largely because to experience the vibrancy of their influence is not part of our education. In the past, however, the temple represented the nucleus of life. All activities within a particular area surrounding the temple would center on the temple, socially, legally and spiritually, so that the concept of religion was more concerned with the religiousness or spiritual nature of life. Law, life and God were intimately connected. We have forgotten these noble values and remember only the trivial and commonplace aspects of the temple.

Temples were placed at the heart of living communities to remind men, women and children that there is another dimension to life apart from the everyday activities of home and work, a dimension that has little to do with markets and desires, but which is equally important for a healthy life – the dimension of God in its broadest sense. This chapter analyzes the influence of a sacred place, the shapes of the "sacred-field," and brings unexpected examples of the phenomenon both in past and present religious traditions. It also refers to *walking* or human temples and their influence. The great enlightened Master, Mahavira, for example, denied the necessity for structured temples, but invented instead a series of positions that the human body can assume which have the same effect as a temple. Today we call his human temples yogic exercises – and the original intention was to create a field around the yogini.

Perhaps some of the most incredible examples of "temples without walls" are those of pre-history.

THE SACRED IMPRINT

Meditation, perhaps a mystery to us all, is an item of life that will soon be as commonly spoken of as jogging! In the same way as the city dweller yearns for the countryside, so the thinker must ultimately yearn for meditation – for inner peace, for something silent against the constant chatter of thoughts that he must contend with everyday and night.
The realization of the sacred nature of meditation comes to all people eventually, perhaps not in this life, but at some moment in their evolution. Those that enjoy the thoughts and the creativity of the mental faculties must inevitably one day cease to do so. And the moment that this yearning to cease begins, so the life of the spirit is given space once again.

Most of us, at some time during a busy year, yearn for time in the countryside. We envy those who live freely amongst the hills and lakes, with animals and forests close by. City dwellers probably spend a large amount of time wishing they could "get away to the country"!

This inner yearning probably arises from an original imprint of the landscape inhabited by the earliest humans. Before the advent of the city there was nothing else, after all, but the cave, forest, ocean and mountain to *formulate* the very foundation of the human mind. Deep down there in the oldest part of the brain lies this same foundation, genetically or otherwise passed on millennia after millennia to us and our modern yearnings. But that yearning is the remaining trace of what used to be mankind's direct connection with life. We, in our long conditioned separative ideas, have lost touch with that connection.

Mankind was once, and perhaps potentially still could be, a complete whole with his environment. The temples that he constructed were an integral part of himself and as such, if we follow the recent discoveries of *anthropology*, we discover the most awesome temples "sunk" into the very land itself that man once inhabited and which we still have access to.

Recent findings show that humans lived in parts of Europe much earlier than had been imagined. Ancient beach deposits on the British coast of Sussex date from the early Ice Ages: they are as much as half a million years old. Axe heads have been found there. In Kent's Cavern, on the south Devon coast line, our ancestors would have overlooked huge areas of forest, for Britain at that time was not bordered by the sea (the English Channel and the North Sea did not exist then). A joined Europe was laid out before their eyes, bathed in a mild climate which supported vegetarian tribes.

Kent's Cavern is an immense, three-and-a-half acre cave with a thousand yards of passages and galleries where the modern explorer can wander deep down inside and feel the warm temperature, 52 degrees Fahrenheit, which is not influenced by the sea outside. Within this extraordinary temple all the effects of religious worship may be felt – the warmth, the fragrances, the

Human beings are aware of a world because, and only because, it is the sort of world that breeds knowing organisms. Humanity is not one thing and the world another; it has always been difficult for us to see that any organism is so embedded in its environment that the evolution of so complex and intelligent a creature as man could never have come to pass without a reciprocal evolution of the environment. An intelligent man argues, without any resort to supernaturalism, an intelligent universe.
Alan Watts.

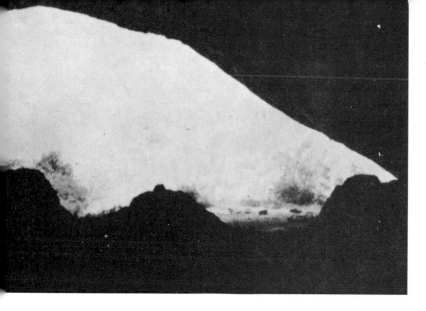

sound of running water and the astonishing womb-like enclosed nature of the cave itself. Today, the entire edifice of this memento of an ancient past is lit with electric lighting but, if the light is turned off, the sensual effects are doubled in their impact and one can actually feel like those who originally dwelt and worshipped there. The rocks themselves are magnificent colors of red, from the iron deposits, and green from the copper.

These were the temples of our ancestors, who had not experienced any separateness from their world. The sounds and smells formed their very religion and places such as Kent's Cavern were their temples of worship – a worship of life itself. A visitor from the 20th century can still find this awe in a few moments of silent meditation. And what is perhaps still more awesome, something we can use as a fulcrum for our modern meditation in these astonishingly sacred places, is the realization that human beings inhabited these caves for 400,000 years!

Here are the equivalents of the ancient Eastern temples, even long before the East became sacred, places where the people thought nothing of possession and lived entirely in the present without desires or dreams of the future and careless of their past – sitting at the beginning of time itself.

The cave paintings on these pages, depicting bison and horses were painted by men and women born directly from Neanderthal man – the "mammoth-hunters" – built like modern man and skilled like modern man.
The horses, for example, opposite, are believed to be a sub-species of the horse, the Chinese Przewalski horse, a wild animal that roamed Asia maybe 30,000 years ago.

The Sacred Adornment of Cave Painting

In just the same way as Michelangelo adorned the ceilings of the Sistine Chapel in Rome, so the mammoth-hunters of 50,000 BC and beyond, adorned, in the most extraordinary fashion, the walls of great caves. They may not have possessed the architectural skills needed to erect artificial temples, but they decorated, with great determination and skill, the insides of their natural temples.

By 50,000 BC the Neanderthal people had largely given way to a new race of humans with much the same characteristics of body and brain as we have today. Modern scholars believe that these people were responsible for the extinction of the mammoth, since these "mammoth-hunters" roamed Europe and left behind them

These paintings survive on rock faces for so long that one must wonder at their permanence. It is as though man has left maps of himself throughout the world molded to the very earth itself. The great chalk figures in England are equally wondrous in their long-standing memory. We can never forget our pagan ancestors.

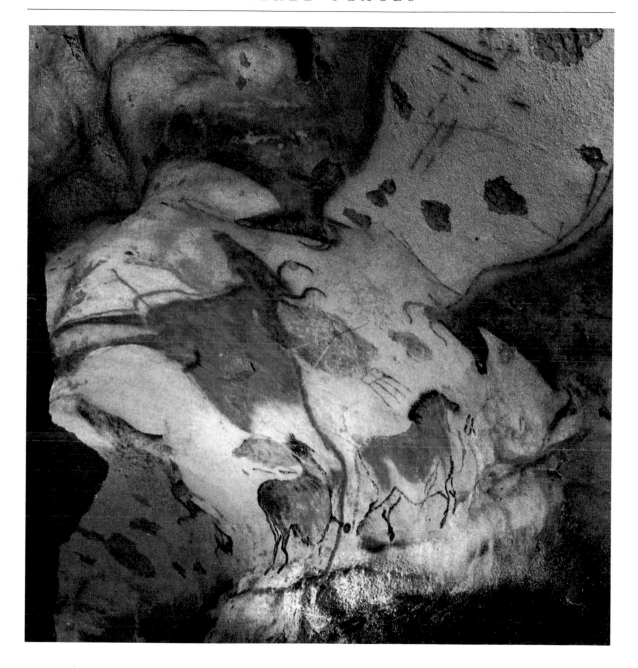

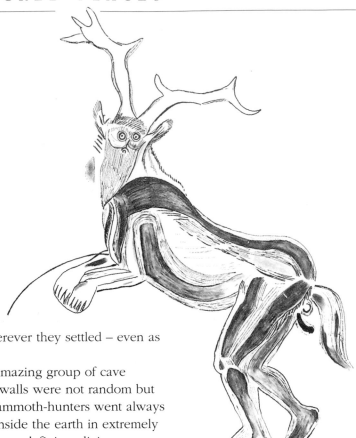

vast quantities of mammoth bones wherever they settled – even as far west as England.

These people also formed a truly amazing group of cave painters and their adornments of cave walls were not random but highly selective. Each generation of mammoth-hunters went always to the same caves, usually deeply set inside the earth in extremely difficult locations to reach. This suggests a definite religious purpose in the creation of these natural temples of worship. In order to reach these holy shrines it was necessary to take long underground river journeys followed by almost impossible underground tunnels, almost too small for a human to wriggle through. Within such caves, once reached, there are still the perfectly preserved footprints of dancing people, impressed into the ground which has, over the millennia, become like stone.

One of the most celebrated of these caves in Europe is called Les Trois Frères, where caverns contain vast halls with painted and engraved representations of animals – hundreds of them in all. The bison paintings and engravings were, it is believed, carried out between 35,000 and 10,000 BC, a most prolific period for cave paintings. In one of the caverns of Les Trois Frères, however, there is witness to the fact that such caves were used as sacred sites for astonishingly long periods of time: underneath the paintings of bisons we can still see the representations of the mammoth painted there thousands of years before.

At one end of this sacred place is depicted the world famous Sorcerer from Les Trois Frères, the earliest known painting of a human being.

An eerie thrilling picture, with his large dark eyes he gazes at the visitor. It is impressive, it is even alarming to look steadily into those eyes which for millennia have stared down from a height into vacant space. This shaman wears upon his head the mask of a stag with its antlers. Bear's paws cover his hands and a horse's tail hangs from his waist. One leg is raised in a dance...Magic and wizardry had their holy place in the Ice Age, places where beasts were enchanted and by supernatural means brought under the power of man. H.Kuhn, *The Rock Pictures of Europe.*

Other shaman or magician figures are painted in other caverns within this dramatic shrine to the ancients, all depicted in dance positions similar to the ceremonial dances that still take place in Africa today.

These caves were shrines – sacred places – visited by the shamans in secret and private sessions, to increase their power and their magic and to keep their contact with the life of their world. In effect, the shaman figures on the walls were the gods of these people, and when they took on the costume of their gods they became gods themselves in their divine connection with life.

These are sacred places indeed. We consider our own temples, the cathedral at Chartres, Stonehenge, Lourdes, to be ancient places of sacred worship – but they are a few thousand years old at most. If that is the case, then these caves within Les Trois Frères are more sacred still, for they have indulged the worshipful energy of mankind for over 50,000 years!

Something we may today find hard to accept is the combination man/animal that dominated the tribes of more than 30,000 years ago. The shaman or tribal witch doctor was depicted as part man and part animal – perhaps several animals – and there were certainly those who believed and still do today, that the shaman was actually capable of making this transformation – this anima metamorphosis.

The "Sorcerer" shown on the opposite page, is a reproduction of the famous cave painting in *Les Trois Frères*, where the walls of stone are so old in the history of man's ancestors that the paintings overlap one another, the top pictures predated by paintings beneath them.

THE SHAMAN AS TEMPLE

The earliest known priests of human life were the shamans. Much interest has been engendered this century in the existence of shamanism, for it is today becoming more relevant to us, as a result of our increased fascination with modern gurus and the slow decline of organized religion. We no longer enjoy the same passion for an outside God who stares bleakly down upon the human race in judgment and remains separated and unconnected to our existence. We are becoming rapidly aware that perhaps the existence of religion and godliness rests within our own personal experience. For those who have had any contact whatever with the modern Eastern Masters, questions inevitably arise as to the whereabouts of the soul and the presence of sacred existence; the

The shaman has taken many forms down the centuries – Merlin, for example – being one of the most famous witch doctors and magicians of any age. His wisdom, enlightened magic and power of healing were both notorious and fascinating, enough to give him power over whole kingdoms.

Modern versions of the shaman still dominate our world – still cause chaos and concern, love and hate. Rajneesh, for example, was one of the biggest thorns in the side of the Reagan administration for more than four years, with his magical recipe for love and growth – magic for some, but evidently not for others! Such is the force of the shaman, for he goes against the norm and stands only for truth.

answers indicate that the old heaven is no longer "up there," somewhere beyond our reach, but right here in our everyday lives.

The shaman was a specialist in sacredness. He was able to meet the gods and take part in the highest of spiritual activities. He was a healer who had the power directly to control and create health and sickness. He was a perfect representation of human spiritual endeavor. He had to attain to complete purity and ecstasy which gave him the power to act spontaneously and always correctly. Bearing this in mind, we can see our modern Masters in the same light. Such well known modern enlightened Masters as J.Krishnamurti, Osho, Meher Baba, Satya Sai Baba and others can be seen as our own shamans with their power to "see" directly into

And beyond all the other areas of mystical understanding is that of enlightenment. Speaking, as we have, of the gurus of today, we might reflect on the whole history of physical transformation, for perhaps enlightenment is nothing more than a physical wisdom that occurs through some natural process which we normal humans can never comprehend. The thousand-armed, eleven-headed Avalokiteshvara, right on this page is depicted from 19th century A.D. China. The story behind the picture is that the Avalokiteshvara, when looking down upon the suffering of the world was filled with such compassion that his head split into eleven parts while many arms sprouted to help with a wise-eye in each palm.

Throughout all the mystical philosophies there is the same resounding theme – compassion and desire are two different things – the first brings true love and enlightenment and the second brings only misery! Such is the fate of the unsacred!

the spirit of mankind and provide "cures" for the modern psychological and physical ills.

The shaman healed the spirit of his tribes, tying together the connections between the inner and outer self. And as such he was a temple of god himself, a walking sacred place.

Evidence within the ancient caves of France and England shows further connections with the modern guru. Within the walls of the cave at Pech-Merle and those of the Pin Hole cave in Derbyshire, there are figures, known as "anthropomorphs," who display features that give the full impression of some transformation taking place. The figures seem to be neither male nor female and have a distinctly disturbing aspect. They are sometimes part animal, part woman and part man, and as such it is believed today that these may have been representations of the shaman in the act of transformation or transcendence to an enlightened state.

The reports today of the physical transformations that have taken place during the process of enlightenment undergone by modern Masters such as Krishnamurti, echo these strange shamanic cave paintings. We may imagine, although we are still lacking substantial evidence, that the physical process of enlightenment is not so unusual in our long history of sacred activity. Perhaps there really is a different state for man to enter, an altered state of consciousness available to many or all of us.

CHAPTER 2

TEMPLES
OF THE SUN AND MOON

CATCHING THE LIGHT

It was once believed, even as recently as the 1970s, that the first race of people to understand the movements of the sun, the moon and the earth and their relationship to one another, were the Egyptians in their building of the Pyramids. But since the advent of carbon dating processes it has been confirmed that long before these people, others of a seemingly less romantic nature had mastered the solstices in a most poetic and dramatic form. Sites of stone-built temples have been examined in recent years to reveal that they were built in precise positions to reflect the summer and winter solstices so that the rising of the sun and the moon on these particular days formed light-patterns within the

On the previous page is the historical site of Glenmark in South Island New Zealand, a sacred moment under the fiery southern dawn sky, unique in all the world.

And speaking of fiery light, we begin the most ancient of journeys – through the light shafts of the oldest races – older still than the Egyptians – but fully aware of the power of our Sun and Moon to direct the labors of the Earth.

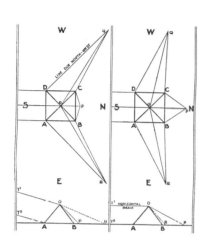

No one today can deny the astonishing powers of understanding and skills of the builders of the ancient past. Even if the earth should shift its axis, engineers have illustrated that the pyramids would still do the job that they were built to do, such is their positioning.

The two illustrations above left show the shadows cast by the Great Pyramid – on the left is the autumnal equinox reflection and on the right midway between the vernal equinox and the summer solstice or midway between the summer solstice and autumnal equinox reflections. These precise shadows were created to indicate to farmers when to plant and grow and reap their harvests.

But this was not new knowledge. It had been around since long before. It is believed that those who learned it first were in the islands of Ireland and England.

entrances to the temples in such a way as to herald the coming of the seasons.

As early as 7,500 BC Ireland was peopled by communities who were, according to modern carbon dating, well ahead of the rest of the world in terms of their understanding of the movements of the sun and the moon. By 4,200 BC they had built the first megalithic (huge stoned) burial passage at Carrowmore, which was followed some millennium later by Newgrange, perhaps the most celebrated and enigmatic sacred monument on Earth. Scattered across Europe, from Scandinavia to France and from Germany to England, there are numerous causeway camps, barrows, henges, "cursus" and passage graves which were left by the tribes and communities of western and northern Europe, all with a strong religious content. This is born out simply by the astonishing effort that went into their building, in some cases it took years with the labor of hundreds of people who would work exclusively at the building of that monument. Durrington Walls in England is said to have taken a million man hours to build.

Our attitude toward Earth was healthier when we were pagans who believed that spirits resided in everything.

The pagan beliefs that created the determination to erect such monuments as the standing stones of Carnac in France, were deeply concerned with the moon's power to change the seasons and influences of Earth's climate and life. Sacredness contains elements of "complete" mystery.

Earth - Man - Earth

Let us envisage the life of Stone Age man in this region of the world: with only a very rudimentary form of agriculture, the land was largely forested and the settlers would hack their way into a clearing within the everlasting areas of oak, birch, pine and elm trees. Amongst these dense forest areas there was marshland and connecting rivers, so that settlements communicated by the waterways and through pathways cut amongst the trees. The marshlands were very dangerous, with venomous snakes and quicksands, and the forests were full of bears, boars, wild cats and wolves which would prey on the settlers. This extraordinarily intense life was surrounded by the silence and the perpetual presence of the dark, green forest.

There are very few places in the world today where we can possibly simulate such conditions. We can perhaps go to a local forest and walk deep into its center, but there are unlikely to be wild bears to give us the sense of foreboding, the primitive uncertainty that must have constantly haunted these settlers. The Black Forest in Germany perhaps comes close, or certain forest areas in Italy where wild boar still roam freely, though there is probably more danger here from the hunters than the animals!

However much we might attempt to duplicate the lives of Stone Age men we can never quite feel either their oneness with nature, their close awareness of the sounds, smells, movements of life, or their natural meditation and religious awareness which must have arisen both from that closeness to life and from the green darkness and silence of the forest areas. And it is likely that out of this religiousness came the sacred monuments that we now find so fascinating.

Until quite recently we did not have a clear view of what the ancient burial mounds were for. They were thought simply to be the tombs of dead warriors of the past. But investigators during the last few decades sat patiently watching the arrival of light shafts into the entrances of the burial chambers and were shocked and delighted to see paintings and surfaces emblazoned in ways that indicated the intentions of the original builders. These places were much more than places of death – they were also places of intense life.

NEWGRANGE

Ireland would have been almost unrecognizably greener five millennia ago, with the greater part of the land still covered by forest. Shortly before the River Boyne meets the sea there are three very unexpected and truly extraordinary sacred monuments which command the valley where they have stood all that time. They still contain the power that was perhaps given them by their original builders and are today known as megalithic mounds or "passage graves". A passage grave is named as such because it is simply a grave at the end of a passage.

Newgrange, Knowth and Dowth are the largest of the clutch of monuments but below them stand a number of smaller mounds and stones. Newgrange itself is surrounded by the remains of a stone circle which was built with exactly the same diameter as some of the circles at Avebury in southern England. At the

entrance to the grave of Newgrange stands a decorated stone: originally it was used to seal the passage but now it stands to one side, where it was moved at some point. The opening reveals a sixty-two foot passage which leads to the center of the mound itself; on either side there are upright stones supporting the roof stones which increase in height as they reach the far end of the chamber. The chamber itself is covered by a corbelled roof which rises to twenty feet above the ground and at its very top is a single capstone. Opening off the central part of the chamber are three burial rooms. The whole structure instills a sense of awe in the visitor.

The single most revealing aspect of Newgrange as evidence of a sophisticated religious people is the fact that at the equinoxes of the year the mounds were used to judge the agricultural changes of the seasons. At particular dates the act of drawing back the door of the mounds causes light to enter the passage and stream down to sweep across the center of the chamber, filling it with the light of the low, rising sun. In the other three surrounding chambers there is an added revelation, for the morning light enters at the equinox and it reveals the elaborate and beautiful wall-paintings in the back recesses. These paintings take on a new life when they are bathed in the light of the rising sun. It is almost as though these paintings were created with this intention, and the sunlight was the artist's assistant, for they only really come alive once the correct day of the year is reached.

In Newgrange itself, on the morning of the winter solstice a window box becomes evident: it was placed by the original builders into the roof of the entrance, and it allows the sun's rays to reach the end wall and thus illuminate carved spirals and shapes on the walls themselves. These carvings include discs shaped like the rays of the sun which cannot be seen as effectively at any other time of the year.

Apart from the fact that devices such as the ones at Newgrange

are evidence of a remarkable skill at measuring the height of the
rising sun, thereby giving the farmer a precise knowledge of the
harvest and planting seasons, the other interesting aspect of these
mounds is that they reveal the fact that Europe was the first to
build and understand something which was previously believed to
have been discovered in ancient Egypt and the Middle East.
Newgrange was built before the Pyramids and even before the
Great Temple of Amon in Karnak where light beams also reveal
the position of the sun in the same fashion.

As well as catching the light of the rising sun during the

equinoxes, these monuments also take advantage of the light shed by the full moon. The contrasting form of light from the moon creates a silvery, fine and almost ghostly presence within the burial mounds and it seems now to the majority of archaeologists that these mounds were constantly in use for ritual processes connected to seasonal fertility and other pagan religious practices.

If we are not convinced of the sophisticated power of these builders of sacred temples after one visit to Newgrange and its surrounding circles then it is only because we of this century have almost completely lost touch with a religiousness that survived for

The picture on this page depicts Bryn Celli Ddu, a passage grave and henge in Anglesey, typical of the burial mounds that can be found throughout England, Ireland and France.

far longer than any we are familiar with today – a religion that was directly connected to the earth, the sun and the moon.

But Newgrange, Knowth and Dowth were not simply built for measuring the positions of the sun and moon. Much smaller structures could have more easily accomplished this task and Newgrange was created from two hundred thousand tons of stone! Imagine a small community of people in a remote valley in Ireland, five thousand years ago, building such a place. They did not do it only for practical purposes or simply to bury their dead. There was a much grander aspect to these temples for they represented the earthly centers for the magnificent worship of the sun and the moon. Man in these times had a far stronger and more authentic understanding of worship and religion than so-called "modern man" has had during the past two thousand years since the rise of Christianity. The worship of sun and moon was directly related to life itself: the sun was the life-giver and the moon was the Earth Goddess. These people were concerned with life, with its formation, its survival and its connections with death and rebirth. Our own view of their pagan and "primitive" behavior is belied by the reverence and power of their connection with that life and death cycle, and we need only enter the burial chambers of these ancient monuments to feel once again the greater strength of our ancestors' understanding of religion – greater by far than any which has arisen since. The coming of science and technology –

The King's men stand silent in the dawn light as they have done for countless centuries, never changing, always there. Their presence is the most sturdy of reminders that we are born from people who knew all there was to know of God.

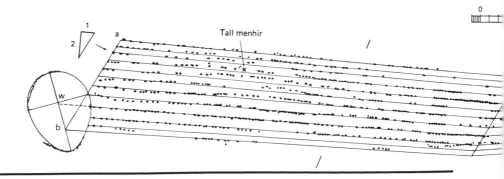

Seen below on this page are the extraordinary alignments of the standing stones at Carnac.

the "age of reason" – has destroyed much of the wonder and magnificence of the sun and the moon, for today we believe that we "know" them and therefore have lost our reverence for them. As such, we have also lost our power of sacrality, for the knowledge we own is on such a superficial level compared to the understanding and depths of ancient Stone Age man, that we can rarely if ever empathize with him sufficiently to comprehend the power of his religiousness.

If we look again at Newgrange and the many other similar mounds, in the light of the worship of sun and moon and earth, we see a different picture. The passageway to the chamber would have represented the birth passage down which the rays of the sun would have penetrated to the central chamber – the womb – where huge mounds of earth were piled up to create the appearance of the pregnant body lying flat on the ground. Anyone buried in such chambers would have been assured of rebirth, as the yearly seasonal light displays rushed into their last places of burial, giving new life each time.

The agricultural seasons were the same cycles as those of man himself, birth, life, death and rebirth, so that the connection between the individual or group human life and that of the land and its life-giving crops were more than simply understood – they were lived.

Man was the earth was man, one and the same.

100m

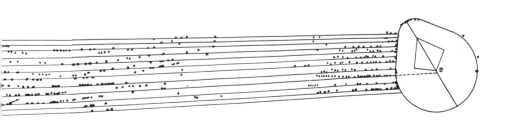

SILBURY AND AVEBURY

Between the time when Newgrange was built and about 2,500 BC there was a tremendous increase in the creation of religious monuments in Europe. There are so many "causeway camps" and other earthworks scattered throughout the Atlantic and North Sea coasts of Western Europe that archaeologists are often unable to account for the many religious persuasions that might have brought them all to life, for it is evident that they were not all created by one concept of belief but many.

The most dramatic of these camps and earthworks is that in Wiltshire, Western England, called Silbury Hill – a 500 foot diameter, 130 foot high hill that is visible from miles away in all directions around it. According to the archaeologist Richard Atkinson the mound would have required eighteen million man

In the Isle of Lewis, the Outer Hebrides off the coast of craggy Scotland, stand the stones of Callinesh. So far from anywhere this isolated, grim and disturbing place was once occupied by a race of people who etched their beliefs from the rock and erected their strength from the ground. Simply to stand amongst the circled stones is enough to sample their feelings.

hours to build and could therefore have taken generations to complete – perhaps hundreds of years!

Silbury Hill is a "harvest hill." Built in the shape of the belly of a pregnant body pointed towards the sky, with a central cone of stone embedded at the very base of the hill, representing the womb itself, its function was to represent the Goddess Earth's powerful and bisexual fertile strength for harvest and survival. Within the hill itself were found a pregnant goddess, an Eye Goddess, a cosmic egg, a sickle, grain and cornstook, a throne, a stag, snakes, a woman with a phallus and breasts, all representing the same earthy, pagan religion that we have already seen in Newgrange.

In the same area of England, probably built at the same time,

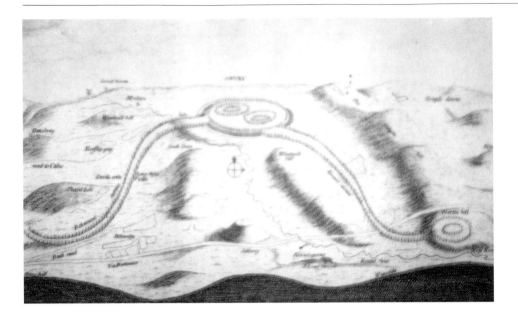

lies also Avebury – one of the world's most beautiful and serene temples, a memento of a religious past that we could well emulate today. The author has spent some time at this monument and in company with many others, has experienced feelings of a deep and profound nature that have never occurred in any "modern" church. The most exceptional aspect of these circles and monuments is their combined power of religion and magic. It is almost as though spells have been cast within the circles that remain available today to those willing to accept their influence. Lying or sitting within the circles of Avebury one can literally be transported into realms of trance which can even become somewhat frightening in their effect, taking the adept somehow out of the body and into experiences that are not at all familiar. It is no wonder that religious groups as recently as the 60s and 70s have used these places, and others such as Stonehenge, to attempt to enact ritual practices in order to emulate the power of religious rituals of the distant past. The power of these temples still exists within them.

The great stone serpent of Avebury, its head, destroyed by the dreadful "Stonekiller" Robinson in the eighteenth century, rested on Overton hill. It is here drawn by William Stukeley before the damage was done. Still today to stand within the circle is to experience something unique and inexplicable.

Avebury is considered to be the greatest of the British stone circles – numbering nine hundred in all – though sadly it was wantonly damaged in the eighteenth century by a local maniac farmer named "Stonekiller" Robinson, who evidently considered his own religious prejudices to be of greater value, and hired thugs to destroy the stones. The eighteenth century Church also had a hand in the destruction. Nevertheless, what remains is still something not to be missed.

A hundred huge sarsen stones were originally erected, only a few of which remain, within a surrounding bank, fifty feet high. Within the sarsen circle were two more inner circles, one on the south and one on the north side, with two lines of stones leading into the circles; of these, one still stands, while the other is totally gone. The surviving avenue of stones is West Kennett Avenue which goes to the Sanctuary on Overton Hill, where "Stonekiller" did the greatest damage. The missing avenue is named Beckhampton; what survives of the Sanctuary is a circle of stones and the still more ancient circle of postholes which once formed a timber roundhouse.

Detailed engravings of the entire complex exist, thanks to a man named William Stukeley who made them prior to the eighteenth century destruction; from these we can see many details, including the shape of the lost avenue which made a serpentine formation as it came into the central chamber – the womb of Avebury. The entire arrangement of Silbury Hill, Avebury, the avenues, and others of this complex formed a tribute to the Goddess of these times. Silbury was the Harvest Goddess who gives birth to the land and to man, while the lost Beckhampton Avenue in the shape of the snake/phallus entered the vulva of the womb of Avebury to give fertility. Avebury signified the Goddess

The picture on this page, looking almost like a photograph, depicts Avebury largely undamaged, and opposite we see the real picture as it is today from surrounding hills. When it was built and for thousands of undisturbed years, this unique monument signified the fecundity of the Mother Earth, the womb, the Goddess and the bride of life.

Man's understanding of his ground was directly associated with his need for what it produced. All religion was connected to the earth for She provided food and shelter and Avebury was one of the largest and most ambitious of monuments to this connection with reality.

as bride and the womb of her conception, a temple of life.

There is no doubt that to visit the whole Avebury and Silbury Hill complex is to find something truly unique and satisfying, for the sacred element and the ancient pagan magic still survive here.

The power of this sacred place is also a reminder that it was built with the full knowledge that the earth which contained it was also of the greatest sacredness. The people farmed upon the belly of Mother Earth under the power of the sun and moon, and their appreciation of these natural and awesome powers was the center of their religion and the reason why they appreciated life so fully.

STONEHENGE

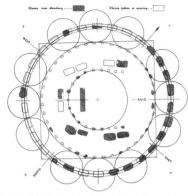

The circles of the New Jerusalem diagram, drawn with correct dimensions as at Glastonbury, define the measurements of the concentric stone rings at Stonehenge.

"The bluestones (were) brought by Merlin from Ireland, having come from Africa in the hands of giants who were magicians."

John Sharkey

Although there is no shortage of books and information about the most magnificent of the circle temples, we cannot mention Stonehenge without stressing its importance.

Stonehenge was not created in one stage but in three. The first Stonehenge was made up of a circle of fifty-six holes, some with bones and some without; this circle was surrounded by a six foot wall made of earth and all this was built around 2,800 BC – 4,700 years ago.

The holes were apparently never used to house stone posts but were filled with chalk, set out very accurately along a circumference with a diameter of exactly 284 feet, showing an error within the circle of only a few inches. Perhaps the most fascinating aspect of the mathematics employed to create this and other circles is that we do not have any idea how the people of the Bronze Age ever worked out the circumferences – the same measurements used in all the circles – even though there appears not to have been any written record that could have been shared by the builders in different parts of Europe.

The measurement used was consistently the same – known as the "megalithic yard", 2.72 feet – and the positioning of the chalk-filled holes is thought to have been set out in order to measure the different phases of the moon over a 56-year period, allowing thus

Stonehenge is still more dramatic even than Avebury and to many forms the most potent of magical stone circles in Europe. Still today there are many visitors, though damage in recent decades has caused the authorities to exact a greater protection to the stones.

This drawing depicts the henge as it was built with everything totally intact, built between 4700 and 2800 years ago. Scientists have still not yet quite fathomed how the stones could have been brought from such great distances as they evidently were.

for all the different positions of the moon in its 18.61 year cycle. Although Stonehenge is now considered to be a sun-worship temple, archaeologists believe that it was originally for the worship of the moon or Mother Goddess.

Some 500 years after the first Stonehenge was built, a second Stonehenge of eighty-two "bluestones" was created from stones transported along rivers and land from the Prescelly Mountains in Wales, about 240 miles away. Each stone weighed more than four tons! The stones are all gone now but archaeologists are satisfied that they were organized into a circle of sixty stones with two horseshoe shapes inside the circle.

Man & the Power of Stone

Once again it seems quite astonishing that these people would have gone to the trouble of bringing such massive stones from so far away, especially considering the difficulties of transport in those times – roughly equivalent to builders today bringing four-ton stones from the moon! – in order to create a stone circle in that particular spot. Religious and sacred values can be the only explanation for the use of such energy. Perhaps the special blue stones were situated in a mountain that inspired strong spiritual beliefs – the entrance to the next world – and the site on which the circle was built was essential in that position for numerous reasons that we no longer really comprehend, such as astronomical values, water dowsing effects and ley lines. The Bronze Age people were clearly very much attuned to the physical universe and their knowledge of how it worked and how it affected man was far greater than ours is today.

Stonehenge three was built around 1700 BC. It was at this time that the bluestones were removed temporarily and placed in careful preservation until the major new part of the monument was set up. And here again we can feel nothing but astonishment at the determination and effort put into the task. Seventy-seven gigantic stones, weighing between 26 and 40 tons each were brought from some twenty miles away. These sarsen stones were accurately positioned according to astronomical observations, slotted into the holes made for them using ropes and pulleys, rollers and men. There were no trucks or power tools or cranes to lift the lintels that were heaved onto the tops of the stones, and they had previously been rubbed smooth, specially tongued and grooved to fit into place as part of the circle. All this was accomplished by human muscle power. Once this new circle was finished, the bluestones were put back in place inside.

It has always been a source of great interest to writers on Stonehenge that it was such a massive and highly accurate astronomical observatory, so much so that perhaps the religious and sacrosanct nature of this temple has been somewhat

The measurements of the circumferences of the stone circles was worked out with great precision and science today still has not figured out what techniques could have been used to do this precise task. Not only this but the same circumferences were employed in many different circles in far off parts of the country so that some communication must have existed amongst people living hundreds of miles apart.

neglected. As Anne Bancroft comments in her book *Origins of the Sacred*, a wooden observatory would have worked equally well and been much easier to erect. Our problem today is that we do not fully appreciate the nature of the sacred as these people evidently did. We have lost touch too much with our connection with the Earth and the pagan senses that were part of life before science and the plague of division. It could have been that there was a fine and subtle puzzle of parts at work in these massive stone circles – a puzzle that contained astronomical observation, stone magic, an awareness that earth herself was a power that needed centers of attraction, the magic of the infinite circle, meridian contact for ley lines under the earth and numerous other parts, all working in a combination of wholeness that we can no longer appreciate. Our understanding today is too fragmented to get to the core of such an operation. If we were to build Stonehenge now we would certainly have all the engineering and scientific potential necessary, but our hearts are in a different place today and the same magic would not be achieved.

Stonehenge was built before the Pyramids and so, at that time, must have stood as the very greatest and most impressive of power-temples on the planet, perhaps considered as the button to be most readily pressed by the cosmic energies that surround this planet.

THE CONE OF SILENCE

In recent times scientists have been taken aback by a response that occurs within stone set up during that period apparently for observatory purposes. They have discovered that the stones themselves during the early morning sunrise respond to sonic equipment with vibrations that can be properly detected, and which die down as the dawn sun climbs into the sky. Geiger counters also register unusually high radioactive output in the circles. And it is solely the stones that are responsible for this sound output. Not only this, but during certain times of year – the equinoxes – the stone circles create an ultrasound barrier.

"At the time of the equinoxes – March and September – the stones emit regular ultrasonic signals. It happens around dawn whether or not the sun is visible and quite independently of weather conditions. As the year draws on towards the solstices, the signals fade away.

But stranger by far, from time to time, the stones create an ultrasonic barrier. A cone of silence on the hillside. This is the weirdest thing. You always have a background of ultrasound in the country – the movements of grasses, leaves rustling, even your own clothing. It all registers. But one morning, as we moved in and out of the circle monitoring the levels, suddenly we found that

Turner's view of Stonehenge as a condenser of elemental forces. The occult mechanism behind its magnetic attraction was considered during Turner's time to be of great significance and recent discoveries have shown that there may be forces within the stones that cause a circle of intense and unique silence at the center.

there was complete ultrasonic silence inside the circle. Our first thoughts were that it was an instrument malfunction. Then we walked through the gap in the stones and there was sound. Inside, silence – outside normal background levels." Don Robins – *Circles of Silence*

Further tests, using infra-red photographic equipment, revealed a light mist around one of the circles in Oxfordshire, called the Rollright Stone Circle, and a ray of light beaming upwards from the top. Such observations are as close as we could imagine to any of the best science fiction stories! The conclusion resulting from these astonishing tests was that these circles are like holes in the landscape. But for what purpose? Was their creation inadvertent? Was it that Stone Age and Bronze Age man did not know what he was doing and by chance made these sacred places with powers that we can today detect? Or was it that ancient man knew very well what he was doing, in fact knew more about the earth and the atmosphere, which incidentally was then totally unpolluted and therefore perfectly clear to the skies, than we know today? Perhaps at this time the people who built such circles as Stonehenge and Rollright could actually see the light mist and the beam to the heavens.

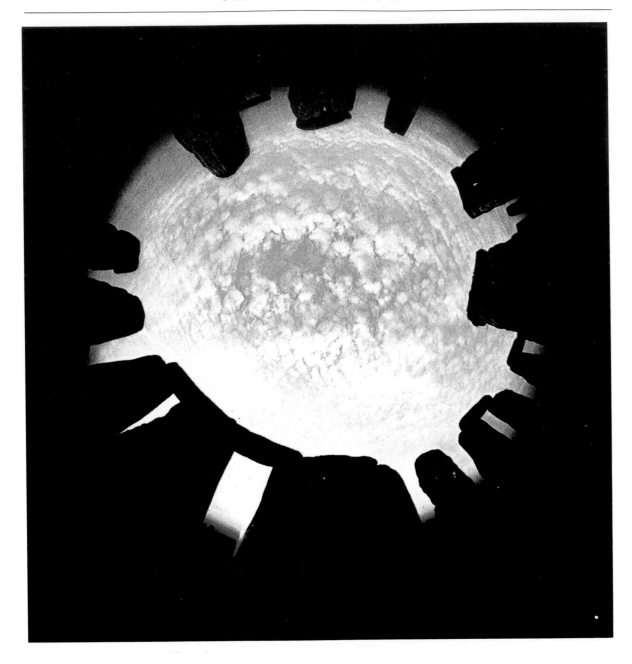

One thing seems sure about the ultrasonic silence within these circles: it must have been a wonderful place for both meditation and an attunement with universal and cosmic energies, both of which would surely have been an intrinsic part of religious and spiritual practices. Perhaps, sitting at the center of a perfectly silent circle of stone, the silence, the circular shape of infinity and the powerful impact of stone on man (the Indo-European word for man and stone are the same), might bring a spiritually sensitive adept into contact with the divine.

But it seems that soon after the completion of Stonehenge the peaceful co-existence of mankind on Earth began to evaporate. The great passion that man had for stone gave way to a greater interest in metal, and with this came a change in the essence of man: harmony and belief in the magical importance of all things gave way to a more stringent and harsher reality which may still be continuing in our society today. Perhaps the Stone Age and early Bronze Age man was the end of an era that created space for another, less yielding and less happy combination of beliefs, and perhaps we are the end of that era. With our renewed interest in the wholeness of life, the New Age and a fresh passion for spiritual understanding, perhaps we are returning to an age that mirrors the peace and beauty of the men and women who produced such magnificent temples of worship as we have seen in these pages.

In any event, towards the end of the Bronze Age when iron was discovered, men's hearts changed and the spirit of humanism declined. We might consider that this period was the very beginning of our time the "killing time" – with war, overpopulation, crowded cities and general strife amongst humans. Before this was harmony and beauty, simplicity and concern within the human community. After it has came almost nothing but trouble – with "the incredible nastiness of man's career upon the earth he has ravaged."

• Perhaps we may see this time, some three thousand years of history, as the painful adolescence of the human race.

The Stone Age of humanistic belief gave way to the Bronze Age, the setting sun falling upon man's understanding of the beauty and importance of his planet. What followed may be considered to be the era of the "killing time" when places like Stonehenge were left to disintegrate while the sun perhaps began to set upon mankind himself.

THE BIRTH
OF EAST & WEST

The Celtic woman passed the rituals and traditions, the land and the wealth to her daughters – not the man to his sons. The rituals were never written, always spoken, for fear of diminishing their power through the inevitable blandness of the written word. Spoken, they carried their original power while the daughters carried their wealth throughout their lives and wore the battle armor beside the men, equally. Equality, in fact, was not an issue but an accepted truth without question and although today we may look back upon these people as barbarians we do so in error for they carried the magic of the world they lived in within their hearts.

THE CELTS

If we search history for the time when Eastern and Western peoples separated and went in two different directions, both geographically and culturally, it seems to have been at the time of the emergence of the Celts in Europe. The Celtic people are thought to have originated around the Caspian Sea and come from a single large group called the Battle-Axe People, from whom the Hindus also emerged. The Celtic speaking tribes moved west through Greece into Europe and the Hindus east into India and Persia, but they seem both to have originated from the same source, though once split they extended into very different evolutions. The language of the Celts, known as Indo-European, comes from the same source as Sanskrit, the classical language of the Hindus, and Celtic gods are seen in the same meditation position as the Hindu gods. The brahmins of the Hindu religion have a great deal in common with the Druids of the Celtic world – both priests drawn from perhaps the same spiritual source. The two groups, however, moved apart after they left the territory near the Caspian Sea, and in almost all ways evolved in opposite directions – the Celts being very tall, fair-haired and blue-eyed, while the Hindus became dark-skinned and dark-eyed with slighter stature. The Celts were known to be magnificent warriors (even the women) and the Hindus spent the greater part of their history, right up until today, being overcome by almost every power in the world.

Despite the fact that the old period of communal spirit of the Stone Age and early Bronze Age peoples had given way to a

battling, separated and egotistical world, the Celts were by no means as narrow-minded and bigoted as most races are today. Women within the tribes were given absolute and legally protected equality. They could chose their own husbands, were protected against male domination and violence, and property was inherited through the female side of the family, not the male. Patriarchy, three thousand years ago had not yet taken a hold on the world.

One of the major reasons why the Celts made such a major impression on Europe between 1400 BC and 500 BC was their ability to smelt and fashion iron. Their presence gave us the name of their age – the Iron Age – and it was their skills that broke the back of peace, for they introduced the wheel and therefore the chariot. They dominated France and England, conquered Rome at one point and even Delphi, and were perhaps the creators of the last great mythical religion, still adhering to the cults of earth, water, fire and the cosmic Mother. Their religion was totally mythical and passed on only by word of mouth, for it was forbidden to write it down.

The very understanding of the spoken word carried with it, consciously or unconsciously, the knowledge that no mythical story could ever successfully be read from a page. The human brain is equipped to accept oral story-telling, with all the human voice's intonations and the visual pictorializing that goes with it. The written word could never carry such power or imagination and this is no doubt the reason why the Celtic people refused to have their private mythology transcribed. This is something that

At the top of this page is an illustration of a celtic vase in the shape of a bull, probably also a lamp, from the mound of Sitagroi near Drama in north east Greece from the Balkan civilization of approximately 4500 B.C..

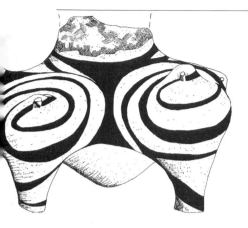

modern education has rarely grasped, with its passion for paper-work and examination, both of which negate one of the deepest mechanisms of the visual cortex and old-brain memory systems. Once again, there is evidence that our ancestors had a greater knowledge of life than we do.

The great power of Mother Earth's stone gave way to the cosmic and diurnal power of metal, largely in the form of iron. Iron had been around for some time but only as derived from meteorite landings. The discovery that iron could be smelted from metals derived from the courses of Mother Earth's deep mines, taken from Her very womb, caused the religious passion for metal to take hold. The smelting process itself was accompanied by the most complex rituals as the miners and smelters of iron ore understood themselves to be supplementing and completing the processes of Mother Earth herself, who might either decide to be benevolent or not. Their reverence was therefore much associated with the concept of death at the hands of their provider.

Celtic practice and mythology was responsible for a great deal of what still remains today, particularly in areas such as Ireland. European cities, such as Paris, gained their names from the Celts (Parisii were a migrating Celtic group) and our modern use of the term "fortnight" comes directly from the Celtic determination of time through the counting of nights rather than days, due to the fact that their highest God "Dis" was a god of the underworld. But most glorious of all the passions that existed within Celtic lore was their appreciation of the sacredness of nature.

Across the bottom of these pages is an ancient Indo-European sculpture depicting the concept of the warrior-king sun as a celestial being drawn through the sky on a war chariot.

Sacred Water, Sacred Wood

The Celtic people were very conscious of the presence of holiness within nature – within a tree, a stream, within holy springs and rocks and grottoes, of which there were many sacred examples. The Great Mother was the guardian spirit who would take care of the shrine employing daily rituals and appearing to the people as a bird or a fish, an old woman or young girl. Very rarely do we find Celtic formal temples like those erected by most other peoples. The Celts were much more likely to build a small shrine within an orchard of trees or on a river bank near to trees, within a natural setting in which they would worship nature and earth without a special building. Strangely, one of the few temples from Celtic times still in existence – over two thousand years old – is a wooden building on the site of Heathrow Airport near London. It

The central concerns of the Celts were associated with the holiness of nature, the trees, the streams and the springs that sprang from the earth. These were their focus of worship. They employed the old stone circles for their rituals and the Druids, their formal priesthood, used Stone Age monuments to gather in and undertake their seasonal worship but they hardly produced any of their own places of religious ritual, preferring the presence of the natural surroundings to monuments.

Temple of the moon – the Stones of
Stennes, the remains of 12 stones in a
circle enclosed by a deep ditch.
Moon worship was an integral part of this
worship for the moon was Mother
Goddess and controlled all movement on
the earth, all crops and seasonal changes.

stands on a site which must once upon a time have been clear of all noise and chaos, in the middle of beautiful countryside!

If we look at the ancient Masters such as Lao Tzu or Chuang Tsu or the Masters of the Indian East, where the Hindu branch of the Battle-Axe people settled, and listen again to their stories, we find a striking similarity to the Celtic appreciation of natural sacredness. One of the most famous stories concerning the "suchness" of existence and the human ability to find it concerned an artist who was commissioned by a famous King to paint a simple reed in the river nearby the palace. The artist told the King that he would need to spend some time with the reeds in order to paint them and after many weeks of waiting the King went down to the river to see what the artist was doing. There, he found him sitting by the river bank swaying in the wind as though he himself had become a reed. The artist told the King that this was so and having found the essence of "reed" there was perhaps no longer any need to paint it!

The Celts found what the Chinese call the "li" of nature – the "suchness", the "isness", the "itness" of life and worshipped with it, in its presence in a far deeper sacredness than can perhaps ever be found by kneeling within a vast man-made cathedral.

At top is a drawing of the hermitage and chapel of St. Michael, Roche in Cornwall England, built into a rock of prehistoric and Celtic sanctity. And below is the holy well, also at Roche, still spouting spring water and a place for throwing lucky symbols.

The Cult of the Druids

It is not possible to look at the Celtic tradition and its sacred places without coming in contact with the now famous "super-shaman-priests" – the Druids. Perhaps because of their origin and connection with their original source – the Hindus – the Druids might be considered to be akin to the past and present Hindu spiritual gurus who we perhaps, if we have had any contact with them, might consider the highest level of spiritual and mystical development on this planet. The Druids were a truly magnificent and powerful form of shamanic priest, with special privileges and the freedom to roam the lands occupied by the Celts, across all borders and through all social structures without restriction. They

At the top of the page are three views of the stone Janus head from Leichlingen in Rhein-Wupper – Druidic symbols that are said to carry magical energy today and often take human form to terrify those that attempt to carry them off.

The extraordinary stone slab to the left was sculptured by the Druid priests as altars for the slaughter of sacrificial victims. The cup-like holes were specially drilled to catch the blood of the victim flowing from the body. In some cases with such stones, the cups were created to allow the blood to flow on and down to the earth while others caught the liquids and retained them for use in rituals.

In some parts of Scotland, Argyll and the Isles, rain water that gathers in the cups and holes of these stones is considered to have curative powers and properties that promote fertility in those that drink it.

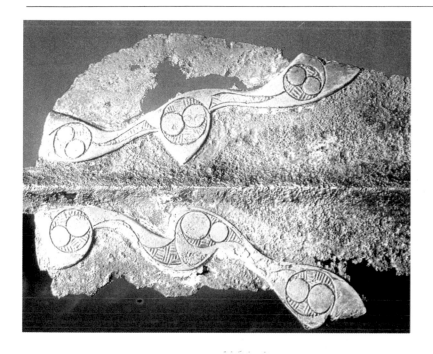

were advisors, guides and judges of almost all aspects of life in those times. They paid no taxes and were, in effect, above the law.

When Caesar conquered the Gallic tribes during the last century BC, the people he feared most were the Druids and their influence continued long after the end of the old millennium right up until the tenth century of this millennium. Their origin goes back in essence to the Ice Age, and they shared the same basic belief as Stone Age man – the concept of three in one: man, earth and god, with a strong connection with animal life and the frequent ability to perform magical feats that could normally only be managed by the animals themselves. Druid priests were thought to advise battle leaders by flying over the enemy and reporting back details that could not possibly have been known except from a great height in the sky. The Druid was protector and founder of the position of King and even responsible for the ritual killing of a King, once his term of sovereignty was completed.

The existence of curative energy within ancient stone has interested even the pragmatic scientists of today. Perhaps stone really can maintain a power within its atomic structure over thousands of years, even perhaps building greater strength as time goes on.

Dowsers maintain that a simple stone or metal piece can echo the past even to the extent of creating emotional responses in those that touch, reflecting past events in the life of the object.

The engraved bronze mounts on the iron spearhead depicted on this page are examples of the balanced asymmetry achieved in insular Celtic art, contemporary to the "mirror style" in the early first century A.D. This piece was found in the Thames River in London and measures some 9 centimeters in length.

The Celts produced, of course, a mass of war symbols. They were a strong, aggressive and warring people and their art went much into the weaponry employed in their conquering ways. Stone was also employed in the carving of warrior statues such as the helmeted warrior on these pages from Hirschlanden in Wurttemberg.

Today we are aware of the Druids, perhaps, only through the annual visit that their modern equivalent makes to Stonehenge, a tradition that has been continued since the Celtic period. Stonehenge was certainly one of their sacred monuments and formed only one of the sacred temples that they made use of. The Druids were concerned largely with the power of the sacred oak groves and the surroundings of their natural world, but they also made full use of all the oldest stone circles and monuments on Earth.

For those who wish to experience the Celtic temple first hand, there are still a few remaining places, the spot where the old King was sacrificed or the new one inaugurated; for example, places where the most intense and powerful shamanic rituals were

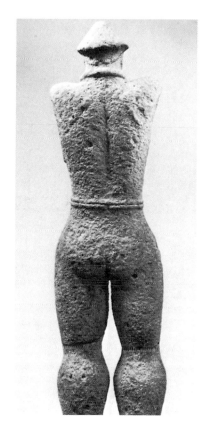

This piece, here seen from two angles, was originally set on the top of a Hallstatt tumulus, looking towards the south-east Alpine and north Italian regions of Europe. It was probably created during the late sixth to early fifth century B.C. and measures some two yards in height. The Sumerian statue on this page is of Gudea – can be found in the Louvre, Paris.

performed and where perhaps the most powerful priesthood of all time enchanted the world of spiritual understanding. Many of these sites were desecrated by the Romans in their search for Druidic wealth in the form of fabulous gold and silver objects, but still today there is a wooden temple at Heathrow, a stone temple remaining at Roquepertuse in Provence, a lake site at Llyn Cerrig Bach on the island of Anglesey which originally contained weapons, bronzes, furniture and ornaments and tools. The same island had originally been the site of the most sacred of the tree groves, which the Romans destroyed in 60 AD. It was here that the most violent acts of sacrifice and killing were enacted so that the very trees themselves would have been stained in blood.

The people of Sumeria were recorders, writing their knowledge of ancient history on stone tablets that have been discovered in the last century. Their stories go back eight thousand years to a people who may have been the very occupants of the Garden of Eden itself. Their sense of elegance and beauty may be sampled from the statues that they left us and their scriptures and records form a remarkable record of a time upon which we have built much of the biblical history which forms the Christian dogma.

THE EASTERN SIDE OF THE COIN

While the Celtic people were developing through the Western traditions of shamanic mystery using the ancient stone circles and temples as their connection with the cosmos, the Eastern arm of the same source was making its progress through India and Persia.

The discovery of the similarities between the two arms of

world population was made originally in 1767 by a French Jesuit, Father Coeurdoux, who observed the strong similarities between Sanskrit and Latin. Sir William Jones, the first Sanskrit expert in the West, also observed during the late 18th century that the connections between Latin, Greek and Sanskrit made it clear that the three languages sprang "from some common source, which perhaps no longer exists."

It soon became clear that there were distinct connections in language throughout the greater part of the civilized world, including the languages of the Buddhist culture (Pali), Sanskrit, Singhalese, Persian, Armenian, Bulgarian, Albanian, Polish, Russian, Greek, Latin and all the European languages except for Estonian, Finnish, Lapp, Magyar and Basque. In effect this meant that there was a continuity stretching from Ireland to India which included also the mythology, literature, religion and form of thought. And most shocking of all for those who were witness to this discovery was the conclusion that the Bible's story of the Creation could clearly not be literally true at all.

But there was one distinct difference between the development of the Celtic peoples and that of the Hindus – the Celts breathed the soul of existence in the very air of their surroundings and paid scant attention to the building of elaborate temples. Their tradition, therefore, has faded faster and left smaller evidence. The Hindus on the other side of the world have built some of the most fascinating and elaborate temples on Earth and these constructions have survived, as evident today as perhaps they were thousands of years ago.

Western man is particularly aware of the Indian tradition today, as he begins to explore through the New Age, the Human Potential Movement and various new forms of psychology and philosophy, the other side of the human coin.

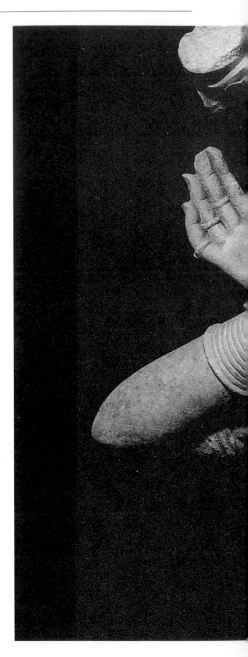

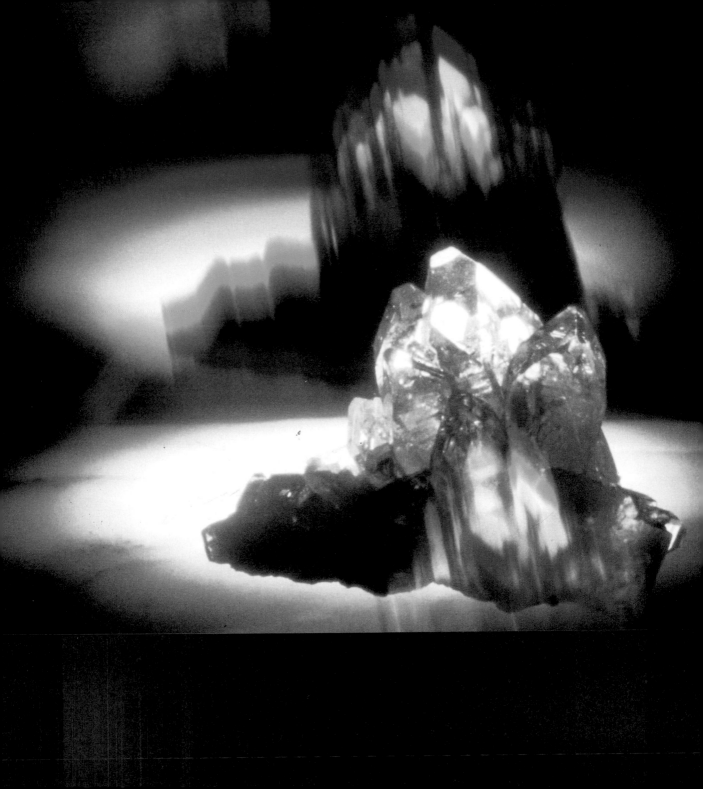

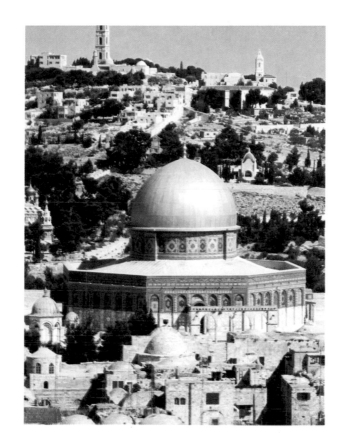

C H A P T E R   4

THE
HOLY LANDS

The coming of Conflict

Until the time of Rome and Greece, Earth's population was small. Figures only began to grow to substantial levels during the latter part of the Iron Age and the result of this growth was the advent of the city. Conflict gave birth to the city. It is as though, already, three thousand years ago, mankind was beginning to jostle for space, even though the figures bear no comparison with today's billions. Vast areas of land were completely uninhabited and whereas during the times of Stone Age man and early Iron Age man, thousands of tribes were scattered across Europe and the Middle East, India, Persia and China, without large centralized grouping, the city developed through a natural process of civilizing which occurred out of a need to

It is hard to equate the beauty and serenity of the city in the hills of the Mediterranean on this page with the understanding that the coming of city dwellings was largely motivated by conflict. Cities were needed to protect and separate the human tribes and peoples that, by the end of the Celtic races, were growing fast in numbers. Cities were often built on high hills to avoid the diseases that frequented the low lands and the robbers that went with them.

defend. Cities were fortifications. It is as though mankind found anger and aggression once he had ceased to be aware of Mother Earth as the founder of all life and the connection with religiousness and the divine.

Nevertheless, the concept of divinity continued. Man did not cease his search for spiritual fulfillment but its form was different. The gods were new gods and the temples were therefore founded on new appreciations of divinity.

In this chapter we will take a look at the holy lands that grew out of the new gods and within those lands, the cities that defended them. And to begin this very brief journey across the globe we start in the most obvious place – the Holy Land itself.

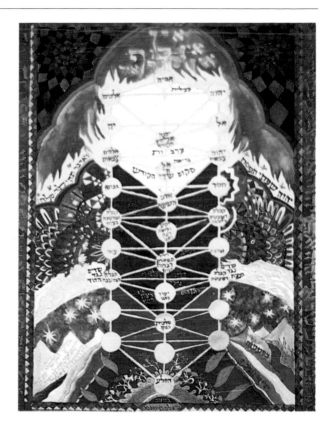

STEPS IN THE HOLY LAND

But still the belief in the mysteries of hidden knowledge prevailed. To know was not to understand and science had taken none of the hold on people that it has today, leaving the wisdom of the Kabbalah as a tradition based in mystery.

The Holy Land is said to have inspired the Ten Commandments, the Songs of Solomon, the Psalms, the Book of Ruth, and, it is profoundly believed, Jesus Himself. Through a series of cataclysmic events the land was molded into dramatically varied forms. The great rift valley that runs from north to south encompassing the "Sea of Galilee", the Dead Sea and the Jordan is a deep cut in the crust of the planet – in fact it is the deepest on Earth that we can find on dry land. The original fissure occurred millions of years in our past but only some eighty thousand years ago the cut in the Earth's surface opened still further and there are some that say that this perhaps coincides with the stories of Abraham, Lot and the Cities of the Plain when God rained

brimstone and fire in all directions. And of course, City of Cities, stands Jerusalem in this Holy Land of lands – the place where David found his kingdom, where Herod created his giant ego on Earth and where Solomon built his first temple. Jesus preached here and here also stands the Holy shrine of El Aqsa, the Moslem temple. As a city it is unique in that it forms a central position for three monotheistic faiths. Jerusalem was in fact, seen as the center of the planet – the Holy Capital of the world – and figured on old maps as such.

On this page is a detail of King Solomon's Temple showing the Ark of the Covenant, the Table of Shrewbread, the Golden Candlestick, the Altar of Incense, the Pillar of Brass, the Louver, the Molten Sea, the Altar of Burnt Offering, the Cheribein, the Tree of Life and the Key Stone, all items of the most intense sacredness that have given life to a thousand myths and stories throughout the ages of Christian religions and their pagan past.

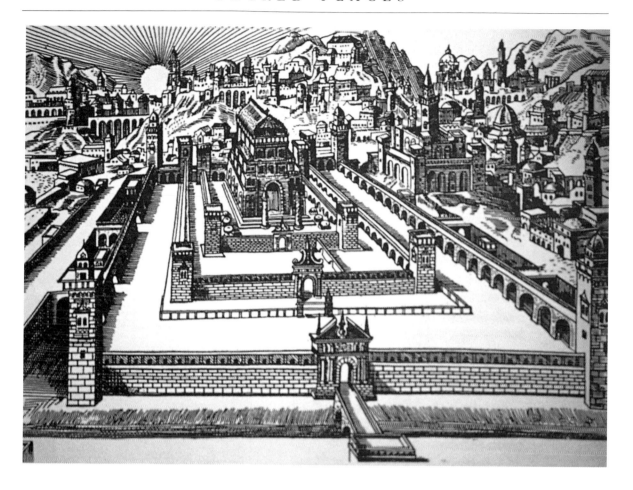

Before Constantine declared himself a Roman Christian, there were hermits in the Sinai desert. They settled there some two hundred years after the death of Christ, choosing it for its sacred associations. It was here that Moses gave God's law to the people and where the Children of Israel wandered for 40 years before entering the Promised Land. These hermits lived in the caves of the mountains until Emperor Justinian built them a monastery and provided them with more lavish accommodation and service. The Monastery, named St Catherine, still stands today like a golden

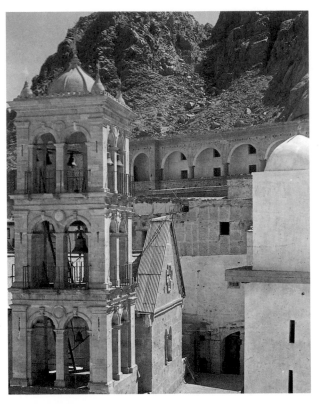

On this spread are various views of St. Catherine's Monastery, a treasure trove of wonder, almost an Aladdin's cave, that has survived since the Emperor Justinian built it for the hermits that wondered the deserts of the Promised Land. Its content of lavish gold and treasure mirrors the gold exterior, standing at the foot of Mount Sanai where it was placed to protect the burning bush in a strategic position for water, a rare commodity in this region.

Also on these pages, top right, is the burning bush altar, beneath, the Church of the Nativity's birth place of Christ and at the bottom the Red Sea surrounding Pharaoh's Island.

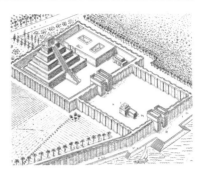

palace at the foot of Mount Sinai where it was positioned to protect the burning bush and because of the nearby water supply. The inside of this extraordinary, sacred creation is quite breath taking with so much richness and atmosphere that a visitor is rendered speechless by what has somehow survived in this arid desert for so long without damage or theft. The place is literally made of gold and jewels and priceless treasures – as rich as Alladin's cave. But St. Catherine's Monastery not only contains treasures of metal and stone but a truly sacred library of some three thousand ancient manuscripts dating back to the Byzantine Empire.

At top of this page is a drawing of the Ziggurat of Nippur – 2050-1950 B.C., dating from late Sumerian times and dedicated to the patron of Nippur, Enlil, the Lord of Air who reigned from the summit of the world mountain.
Below is a rendition of the worship of the Tower of Babel from a romantic nineteenth-century painting.
To Babylon were brought the priests and teachers of Egypt, Palestine, Zoraster, Mithra, Greece and masters from all parts of the known world.
Gregson.

The monks that live in this extraordinary place follow the rules set for them by St Basil – no meat, only fish and much fasting with days made up of prayers and work in the workshops and looking after tourists and other visitors. In this respect the Monastery of St. Catherine is like many others, but there is at least one aspect of this strange shrine which is perhaps not so "standard".

The basis of the beliefs inherent in much of the Christian mystical creed is the worthlessness of mankind's existence on Earth when compared with that which he will transcend to. Heaven is best. In St. Catherine's monastery evidence of this attitude can be directly witnessed in a small chapel beyond the walls of the fabulously embellished structure. Here, hundreds of skulls and bones are kept, piled high. These are the remains of the monks that lived in the Monastery, buried after death and then exhumed after two years and dismembered, the skull being the most important part, piled in preference to the bones which are left in a dishevelled heap. Certain well-known monks have been given precedence and are displayed in special niches with name tags. In a way it is a strange paradox that the monastery is so filled with gold and treasure and the bones of humanity are given less importance, discarded beyond the walls of the Holy Shrine.

On this page is the Colonnade of the temple of Amon-Ra drawn by Napoleon's savants in 1798. Aimed like a telescope, the colonnade and the temple's axis oriented to the summer solstice.
And to the right is the city of Babylon of Nebuchadnessar – 604-562 B.C., this painting a restoration picture by Maurice Bardin.

"The meeting place between heaven and earth – here the divine enters the human world. This we can call Holy Ground."

The past two thousand years, since the disappearance of natural divinity, have so dispersed the sacredness of Mother Earth that we are now hard-put to find a conscious divinity. We hold dear, therefore, the places that manifestly display the sacred. Jerusalem is undoubtedly one of these.

The city with a hundred different names – "Yerushalayim" – in Hebrew, appears in the Bible 656 times and its earliest mention on

record in Egyptian texts, around 1900 years before Christ, calls it "Ushalmes".

The Romans virtually destroyed the city in AD 70 while putting down the first Jewish revolt against their rule. The Temple built by the exiles from Babylon and enlarged by Herod the Great, was almost completely devastated and never rebuilt. The one remaining part still standing today is, of course, the retaining wall on the west side of the Temple Mount. Known to most people as the "Wailing" Wall, it is perhaps the most precious relic of Jewish faith in existence. There are also other, more recently uncovered remains of the Temple Mount such as stairs that rise from the

Delphi – the receptacle of the earth spirit in the clefts and caverns of the ground from which she sprang. A cavern, according to ancient theology, was a gateway to the lower kingdom, a passage for spirits to descend into Tartaros and rise again into the new generations. Cracks in the earth allowed the earth Goddess's influence to lift into man's domain.

The cleft rock from which came the vapors that inspired the oracle at Delphi gave reason to the derivation of the name – meaning vagina so that the cavern became a favorite place for sexual fantasies in modern psychology. The true meaning, however, was seen to be deeper than simple human sexuality and lay as a source of the most powerful and terrifying forces that Mother Earth could inspire. The State magicians of Babylon were initiated underground and it is said that the experience was so terrifying that some never smiled again.

This understanding seems to arise, though, more in the times when religion is not fully understood for the Greeks had no problem with the underground gods and goddesses for they were familiar with their ways and with the "chthonic" element in the spiritual nature.

Lower to the Upper City and these relics inside the very special sanctity of Jerusalem attract the orthodox Jewish community who live in the quarters of the city where strict traditions are maintained.

In these areas the traditional Jewish dress is adopted with black coats and long beards and sidelocks, the women dressed in the old way and the children educated without modern learning.

But not only the old prevails in this wondrous city of religion. Modern architecture is also strikingly present and in particular the "Shrine of the Book", part of the Israel Museum stands out with its curved and elegant roof. Inside is the display of the Dead Sea Scrolls set in a kind of modern cave-like design, the scrolls themselves displayed along a tunnel underneath the dome.

Yamabushi

Yamabushi, depicted on this page, takes us into the strangest and most sacred elements of the Far East. The sacred waters, statues and grounds of this extraordinary location can only be sampled in person. Ontakesan, the mount of paradise, seems to portray the rising of humanity from the rock itself.

And then, of course, there is the "Via Dolorosa", perhaps the other most precious and holy sites in Christendom. This path was taken by Jesus after his trial, carrying the cross to Golgotha. Along the street there are churches, each representing the dramatic events that Jesus underwent during his last journey. The most dramatic of these is the Church of the Holy Sepulcher where the last five events are represented and where the Christian sects of Greek Orthodox, Roman Catholic, Armenian, Coptic and Syrian are all represented. On any sacred search, this church has to be a stop along the way for its extraordinary flavor of religious passion and riches mixed from the various persuasions, makes it entirely unique.

To be the oldest city in the world Jericho, or the site on which it stands, would have to be dated somewhere more than 10,000 years ago. In fact a history of the surrounding area has been discovered near to the modern city of Jericho which names a habitation dated between the 9th and 11th millennia BC at a time when a prehistoric culture of "Natufian" people occupied the area. The people were semi-nomadic and pagan in their religious beliefs, living in huts and presumably part of the global Earth-connected belief system that we examine in other parts of the book. Records also exist here of Neolithic settlements in the 8th millennium BC with perhaps a small established city of more than two thousand people. The archeological finds have revealed Bronze Age settlements, Canaanite peoples and their destruction by the Israelites who encircled the walls of Jericho seven times and blew their trumpets to bring them down. And since these stories were told the city has continued to thrive with various ages of mankind. There is perhaps more varied and complex energy within Jericho from its spectacular history than in any other city world-wide. But sadly we must move away from the sacred places of the Holy Land in this short section on specific places, and travel to another of the world's most astonishing holy lands – Northern India.

City of Light

Benares is one of the world's most enigmatic sacred places, combining the influences of smell, touch, sound, humanity, water and tradition. There are those who will spend the last years of their life by the river Ganges at Benares, resting there for the betterment of their future lives.

INDIA

There is no way, of course, that we can even begin to cover the wondrous sacredness of this fascinating sub-continent in so short a space. Suffice it to say that wherever a visitor goes, once having fallen in love with India, there is a special atmosphere beyond the poverty and the dirt that lies everywhere, that will remain forever in the memory, perhaps in the soul.

Most Indian sects spend some time on Mount Abu, either settling there for periods in ashrams or coming simply to meditate

As Mount Abu is the holy mount for the Jains, so Banares is the Hindu's holy City of Light. Take a boat ride at dawn along the three-mile-long eastern-facing curve of the Ganges river. But it must be early morning – around 5.30 a.m. – and the strange ghostly mist lays languidly on the river. As it clears, so you will see

The Tibetan philosophy of divinity derives from the presence always of color and gaiety and may be influenced also by the benevolent aspect of ritual correctly performed. Prayer is even "advertised" by the presence of flags on the tops of temples such as the picture on the opposite page at the Buddhist shrine in Bhutan, the flags enlivening the spirits of the local area and designed to make them happy.

The native Shinto religion to the area where this shrine stands also nurture a thorn tree hung with strips of paper or cloth as a further attraction to the spirits, encouraging them in a favorable attitude to the welfare of the local people.

the maharajas' palaces, various temples and ashrams and mosques and the wide steps that lead down from them to the river – known as the ghats.

On these holy steps, bathing in the holiest of rivers, thousands of Indians, both men and women, bathe each morning as the first act of the day. The moving waters of the Ganges are perhaps the world's most fluid sacred place and the city of Banares, known still by Hindus as Kashi, the City of Light, is the most potent center for Ganges worship. Watching the river view after the mist has cleared, it becomes patently clear why the place is called the City of Light, for the incredible luminous colors shine throughout the streets and temples as the sun rises directly across the river, flooding everything in golden light.

MAYA

And finally, we pass through Mexico and Peru with a glance at the Mayan temples of the Yucatan – the temples of the Maya and then the great earth markings of the ancient Peruvians.

The Maya conceived the world as having no less than thirteen heavens, one on top of the other in layers, the bottom one being Earth. There were thirteen gods, each one presiding over a single heaven. Beneath the world, there was also the underworld, also

Top left of this page depicts the priest-king Quetzalcoatl, the wind god Ehecatl, in the form of a Mexican body stamp. The very basis for the sacredness of the shaman, witch doctor, magician of all races and creeds was that man could not make magic of his own volition. He needed something very special to take him into communication with the divine.

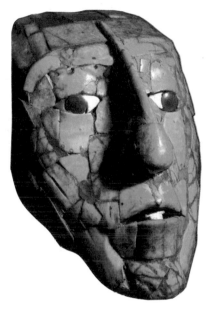

Specially trained and initiated men and women were, therefore necessary to make this bridge.

Such is the belief of the Mayans and the basis for the building of the Palenque Pyramids on this page.

layered in a convenient pile of nine levels, one god ascribed also to each of these layers. The bottom layer of this deep and dark course was "Mitnal" over which ruled Ah Puch – the Lord of Death.

The Yucatan is literally mind-boggling in its range of beautiful, shocking and sacred sites. There are the Mexican pyramids which are virtually man-made mountains, the temples, the castles such as "El Castillo" or the Temple of Kulkulcan. There is the Toltec

Tezcatlipoca had bought a potion, brewed by the magic of the goddess Mayahuel of the agave plant from which pulque is extracted. Pleading illness when the vessel was offered, the god-king declined, but then pressed merely to taste with the tip of his finger, he did so and was immediately overcome by the potion. He then drank the whole contents of the bowl and became drunk with it. Sending for his sister Quetzalpetlatl, he bad her also drink and she too sank to the floor under the influence. Following what he saw as a dread sin, Quetzalcatl burned his palace, buried his treasures in the mountains nearby and turned the chocolate trees to mesquite, telling also his multi-colored birds to fly away. He then departed.

Standing at a rock side and looking back at the favored city he wept and his tears sank into the stone leaving a mark also of his palms there. On the way he underwent various trials and games and the remains of his journeying have formed the basis of the Mayan myths ever since.

Temple of Quetzalcoatl, the Mayan Temple of the Cross. There are so many legends, stories and myths that the visitor can rapidly end up in a trance of sacredness, for the religious power of the Mexican ancestry is not only very strong but labyrinthine in its complexity. But ultimately the symbols and myths are at the same essence as the religions of the West and East, the same heaven and hell, the same reward on the other side. It is as though mankind was built always from the same materials to arrive always at the same place of understanding. The Mayan culture to this extent is no exception but of a very different flavor.

In the great Nazca Desert of Peru there is an earth-marking that was not recognized for what it represented until man had learned to fly. From the ground it is much too vast to be taken in at a single glance but from the air it can be seen to be a gigantic hummingbird laboriously cut into the ground over an enormous area. The discussions as to whether such earth markings could possibly have been done without knowledge of flight, have led to all manner of conjecture about visitors from outer space, of extra-terrestrial helpers and UFOs guiding the artists of the time.

The truth is that modern man has no real concept of ancient man's capabilities, for perhaps they were far greater than he suspects. How many sacred places exist, built in the last two hundred years, that could possibly be compared with anything from the distant past? What do we have that compares with the Yucatan, with Stonehenge, with any of the places mentioned in this book?

C H A P T E R   5

THE ROMAN MIGHT

Rome brought a unique flavor to God. Such was the ego of this extraordinary empire that it sought to "organize" religion. Like almost everything else in Rome, belief was to be subservient to the cause.

Gods and goddesses such as Minerva and Apollo on these pages, stood alongside Alexander the Great, on the chapter title page, self-declared human-god and conqueror of the "world."

One thing, for sure, that can be said about the Romans was their amazing ability to create. There are probably more artifacts and monuments from Roman times than from any other single epoch, each item signifying some aspect of life, each one worshiped for the practical return that it would bring.

Alexander, though, in his determination to become divine during life, was duped, for the priests of the temple of Jupiter Ammon, in which to save their village from his might, performed various suitable rituals and declared him to be the son of the god in residence. As to the mysteries of divinity, they side-stepped the issue by the use of elaborate devices and Alexander left this strange and awesome place none the wiser!

RELIGIOUS ORDER

The Romans, as brilliant administrators, had little interest in the infinite realm of the spirit. Their basis for belief was that of order and command, of a very human and grounded understanding of the divine. Religion was a state affair and related to adherence to the rules of war and efficiency. They could never have succeeded in commanding such a vast empire on Earth had they continued a process of religiousness which was in any way mystical and unknown.

Spiritual commitment is a commitment to upheaval, an appreciation of chaos and the see-saw of constant change. The Roman people needed certainty and order in all aspects of their lives and this can be seen in the manner in which they created

Rome itself, for Rome was a temple to Roman endeavor, the Roman Gods simply enlargements of humanity whom anyone could approach, given simply the pious background of family tradition, adherence to the state and the correct rituals. Anne Bancroft, in her book *Origins of the Sacred,* calls Roman religion, "a shopkeeper religion."

Like almost all imperial nations that have sought to conquer large proportions of the world – Britain, Austria-Hungary – Rome used religion as a stabilizer rather than an inner power of discovery. It was suitable that the people should believe in a God or gods – part of home and hearth – a piece in the puzzle of human needs, no more. The most typical Roman gods were headed by Mars – who had originally been the Italian god of vegetation and fertility who lived in the mountains and forest lands – otherwise called Silvanas (from the word "silva," meaning forest). Mars became the God of war.

The root of the word "Mars" is "mar," meaning to shine, and before the foundation of Rome, the Italians of Etruria and Umbria called him Mars Gradivus, meaning "he who grows" or "becomes big." This connotation, when transformed into the Imperial Roman interpretation changed to Mars Gradi which meant "marcher" and the idea, perhaps, of growing big and shining were appropriated into the warring sense of conquering and and winning over the enemy.

The Roman people spread sacredness, in their own particular form, over a vast area and through a large number of mythical devices. Minerva, for example, one of the three state divinities of Rome, and thus especially honored, presided over numerous holy shrines. She was Goddess of the thunderbolt of wisdom – note that for the Romans wisdom came by so powerful a force – and later became also the protectress of commerce and learning. One of her best known sanctified centers still exists today in England, the springs of Bath where a recent archaeological dig has revealed thousands of coins thrown by Romans as an offering to her into

The central issue within the Roman system of divinity was patriarchy. Men ruled and women advised at best. The holy backdrop of the social environment was no more, in a sense, than a convenient substance designed to engender fear and doubt, a divinity based on a sophisticated form of superstition.

But the Roman leaders, or many of them, were generous to the local beliefs. Once conquered, a people would be permitted their faith, whatever it was and very often the legions of existing gods and goddesses were supplemented by those whom the soldiers met along the way. Thus came the flavor of Greece and later that of the East, as the traveling might of the Empire became bored with the uninspired attitude of Rome to divinity. The East carried something unique, a real flavor of truth, spiritual and absorbing, so that much of the "outside" god was supplemented by an "inside" godliness, a direct link to the universe.

In this way, somehow, the western understanding began once again to merge with the eastern divinity after thousands of years from when the battle-axe people had split into the Celts and Hindus.

the waters. Her identity, like many of the Roman divinities, varied from country to country – in Britain she was Goddess of healing, which explains why she was worshipped in Bath. The Romans were infinitely adaptable, primarily because their interest was to conquer and be powerful. Religion, too, was forced to compromise with local conditions. You could not afford to have a universal God for this meant greater expense at war, since it would become necessary to conquer not only the bodies of the enemy but the spirit as well.

The Goddess Athene, the Greek equivalent of Minerva, may also have been responsible for the very first patriarchal attitude. Zeus, her father, could not allow his wife, Metis, to give birth to Athene and so ate Metis. But shortly after this somewhat gross act, he suffered from the severest of headaches and, presumably in order to relieve him, Prometheus took an axe and split open his head. Athene sprang out from her father's brain – the first male brain-birth – something that in the height of the patriarchal suppression of women, was seen as a genuinely laudable act. Women were, after all, simply useless chattels to give birth to an already perfectly formed fetus deposited there by the male organ! The male brain-birth was an even better idea.

But the Roman religion was, for all its order and glamor,

The cult of Mithra, originally from Persia and the East, was adopted by the Greeks and Romans, to be the concept of the opposites – life and death, good and bad. The pagan nature of this cult epitomizes the differences between our modern interpretation of sacrifice and the original intention which was fertility and growth. Life was within death and vice versa. Good was within bad and the two merged to form one humanity. In this way we cannot fully appreciate the original for we have imposed our own format upon it and thus have become lost in the modern terms of Christian dogma which eventually took advantage of the negative aspects of the Goddesses message.

somewhat boring, and by the first century AD the Empire had reached far to the East and begun to come in contact with a strange culture that greatly fascinated the Romans. It was so different from everything that they were accustomed to. Roman official life included official religion with all its rituals and certainties, whereas the Eastern cults carried a direct relationship between the individual and the divine. The mysteries of the universe were available for personal sampling through meditation, through secret initiations and prescribed conduct, and all this, if followed with care and attention, could lead to fulfillment in this and future lives.

The Cult of Mithra

Over the page on 134 and 135 is a depiction of the temple of Jupiter, now no more than a few standing pillars and arches. The original must have been a truly magnificent sight, standing on the north side of the forum in Pompeii. Only the priests of Jupiter were permitted to enter the central part of the temple and at the back were various statues of the gods, Jupiter, Minerva and Jove. The cellar of the temple contained the wealth of the city and the whole building was erected 150 years before christ.

The famous modern preserved temple, following the volcanic eruption at Pompeii, was in the process of being rebuilt when the lava descended and preserved the workers and people living there to give us one of our most strange and unique monuments to Roman life.

One of the cults that came originally from the East, from Persia, and spread noticeably through the Roman Empire, was that of Mithra. Mithra was the messenger of light sent to Earth as a source of fertility. The image associated with him is the slaying of a bull, who, instead of gushing blood from the wound inflicted by Mithra's sword, pours grain. In Greece during the Hellenistic period, bulls were actually sacrificed and the blood allowed to pour over an initiate who lay beneath the slaughtered animal in a pit, while two men stood on either side of the animal holding torches, one upwards and one downwards, to symbolize the sending of light above and below in the same way as the two thieves, one good and one bad, were symbols on either side of Jesus's crucifixion. The concept of opposites, derived and administered by the Greek dualistic foundation of life, is apparent in this symbolism. Life was opposite to death, spring opposite to autumn, love opposite to hate, etc. The dualism within the Greek context was not perhaps the same as we have adopted it today. Death and life were opposites but they were also within one another. It was not possible to live without death and death could only occur within life. Our fear and passion for the taboo of death during the 20th century has rather changed this subtle understanding for today we do everything in our power to avoid death – as if casting it out of life, instead of embracing its power. In the cult of Mithra, the sacrifice of the bull loosened the knot of opposites, uniting death and life together for those who took part in the initiation.

In this century we are shocked by such "pagan" rituals but truthfully they still go on today, though with less of the respect and passion that was involved in the past. The Spanish bullfight is a vestige of this same ritual, the slaughter of the bull, which was then supposed to be cut up and buried so that the sacrificed animal would ensure the healthy growth of the crops. For the most part the Spanish bullfight is now only a matter of macho madness, lacking the "salt" and retaining only the cruelty. In the rest of the world, the bull is slaughtered in exactly the same way as in the Mithra cults, in every slaughterhouse, each killing lacking even the slightest vestige of respect or religious concern for life.

To the Romans, the greatest fascination of the Mithra cult lay in its initiation rites which effectively gave the individual the opportunity to reach divinity simply through his or her own efforts. There were seven levels to be achieved before enlightenment, the same seven levels that the soul had passed through in order to enter the body of the unborn child. The concept was closely allied to astrological understanding, which had already been outlined more or less as it is used today. The soul passed through the seven planets' visible auras around earth, receiving at each aura some characteristic that would form a part of the struggle and also the joy of the life to come.

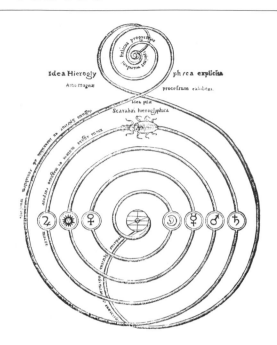

SEVEN
STEPS
TO HEAVEN

The life of the initiate was then a process of passing back through each of these seven stages, redeeming the seven levels of his soul's character until he was finally once again in an unconditioned and blissful state. The process is, of course, very similar to many of the ancient/modern Eastern cults in which the initiate or disciple must pass through levels of inner awareness, to find the center of divinity. The process may be consciously to travel inwards rather than outwards as in the Mithraic cult, but essentially it is the same insofar as the auric levels of the planets were only symbols of the inner journey to sacredness.

The seven levels are succinctly personified within each planet. First came the moon orbit which contained the waxing and waning of life, followed by Mercury which was the aura of rebirth into spiritual understanding and initiation into magic and occult wisdom. Next the disciple passed on to Venus, where passion and the illusions of desire were surpassed – the same concept seen here in our New Age cults where sexuality is transcended – and on

On this page is an illustration, made in the 17th century, of the original Egyptian concept of the seven steps to heaven. Egyptian initiates were named scarabs, after the insects that push their own eggs across the ground while they contain the coming generation. The path of the alchemist is a double spiral representing the alchemist's alternate dissolution and coagulation, the expansion and contraction of the spherical vortex and the phases of the subtle energies. The idea was that the initiate moved through all the planetary spheres until he or she reached the center and enlightenment – pushing the egg of the future generations before him.

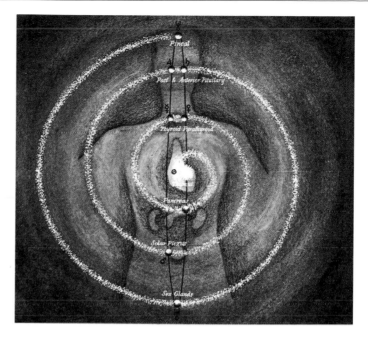

On this page we see the Mithraic cult symbolism in the form of a "Leonotocephalic Kronos". The energy centers of the body, the chakras in Eastern culture, were the adapters and transformers of spiritual growth. The sun and the source of the energy was the heart and the pineal gland formed the "sight" or outpost of the body, for it was believed that this tiny gland in the very core of the old brain center had the power to receive light. It was thus the medical receptor of the "third eye". There is now some modern medical evidence to support this belief as the pineal gland does in fact seem capable of light refraction within this deep set part of the human brain.

to the Sun where the initiate was to face the intellect and a greater understanding and knowledge, thus overcoming the power of the mind. Mars came next, forming the center of courage, perhaps one of the most powerful of changes, and then on to Jupiter where he would have to give up the strength of his courage and overcome fear, relaxing into inner strength. Lastly came Saturn where he transcended all matter and was the "Father", an incarnation of divinity.

Such was the power of this cult that Roman soldiers were the greatest adherents, for the challenge of the Herculean-like stages of transcendence were of the greatest excitement to these warriors.

With the coming of the Christian God, the similarities with the Mithraic cult were so great that the Christians were forced to conclude that Mithra was brought to Earth by the devil to mock their Christian savior, even though Mithra was around a long time before Christ!

Opposite is another representation of the concept of the "subtle body" – that body which exists in a kind of non-physical relation to the "obvious body". The drawing was made in 1820 – Kangra, Himachal Pradesh.

In typical style though, the Christians who had to deal with this subtle doctrine of Eastern understanding, embodied by Mithra, presumed that it had been sent to tax their understanding by the devil, even though Mithra was around a long time before Christ!

At right we see a representation of Dionysus riding the Bull. Once the realization of heaven and hell, being and non-being has been fulfilled, so then the life-joy will pour from everything as though from an everlasting cup. First the ego must be sacrificed and then the realization will return it intact but carefree and everlasting life gushes forth.

This is the mystical-psychological foundation of all religions – the Mayan Aztec, the Hindu, Buddhist, Christian and even the modern religions that are sprouting so healthily today.

Enlightenment is the divesting of the troublesome ego, the dropping of the attention to thought and fear, and once this state has been attained so joy and blissful tranquillity can be attained by the initiate. Go to any of the Indian ashrams – Krishnamurti, Rajneesh, Muktananda – and the same story is told in varying forms, the same story as we have been hearing for thousands of years, fresher perhaps than the now diminishing remainder of the Christian dogmas, but still ultimately the same.

Egypt, Greece and the Gods of Nature

In many ways the Romans can be seen as an interregnum of the divine, for although their military and ordered form of divinity temporarily diverted them away from the more subtle and spiritual forms of religiousness in order that they might achieve the position of the ultimate conquerors, as the power of the Empire waned so the pagan Gods returned in force, helping in the eventual downfall of Roman dominance in Europe and the Middle East. It is also so today, in a similar way. The power of the nations that have striven so hard to form a secure civilization – America, Soviet Russia, Communist Eastern Europe – is slowly now being undermined by a strong new movement back to the disorder of spiritual searching and uncertainty. It is as though man cannot stay away from his deeper, inner functions for long and, however hard he tries to underpin his life with safety, order and security seldom survive for long.

Rome was also attracted by the ancient beliefs of Egypt, particularly in the form of the Goddess Isis who handsomely epitomized the Mother Goddess in all her most evident forms. She was noble protectress, wise administrator, good and loyal wife and mother all wrapped into one.

The Romans also adopted Dionysus, giving him the name Bacchus. Today Bacchus is commonly considered one of the major forces that brought about the degeneration of Roman qualities into drunken orgies of promiscuity, but the true God Bacchus was of greater significance than our superficial interpretation of him. Dionysus/Bacchus was certainly a fertility god with strong connections to the earth, the trees and seasons with miraculous abilities to produce wine from water, cause rocks to gush with milk and honey, but he was also closely, symbolically connected with the Eastern spiritual path in his story. He was first born to Persephone and Zeus – Earth Mother and Sky God – but as a child he was taken by the Titans, who had built the physical world, who tore him to pieces and ate his flesh, leaving only his heart which Athene saved. Zeus burned the Titans with his thunderbolts and created the human race from their ashes, which of course also

On this page is depicted the hold pectoral of the winged Isis wearing the Egyptian symbol of the throne on her head. The piece was discovered in a pyramid in Ethiopia, dated at about 600 B.C. and found now in the Museum of Fine Arts in Boston.
Opposite again is Isis holding her brother and husband Osiris.

contained Dionysus's essence, since he had been eaten by the burned Titans.

His heart was reduced into a love-potion and given to Semele who was in love with Zeus and became pregnant by him. But she could not sustain the fire of Zeus's body and was burned to death, while Zeus took the unborn child into his thigh and eventually gave birth to Dionysus for the second time – birth and re-birth.

It was only later that Dionysus, becoming Bacchus, was credited with discovering the grape and therefore the joys of wine, thus being somewhat denigrated into the self-indulgent orgiastic god. The degeneration of Roman power and the Empire occurred through a softening of the military order and an increased fascination with the divinity of the soul, but perhaps Bacchus helped them on their way with a little sweet wine!

CHAPTER 6

HOLY WELLS
WATERCOURSES & THE LEY

Water everywhere

Water is well-known to Western civilizations as a sacred substance and most of the temples of the West contain holy water as an intrinsic part of the sacred rituals of religion. The presence of water still occupies our modern sacred places and forms the same essence as the fragrances and light, already mentioned.

"As Satan was flying over harrogate wells
His senses were charmed by the heat and the smells!
Said he "I don't know in what region I roam,
But I guess from the smell -that I'm not far from home!"
An old Biddy called after him "Satan, I say!
You seem mightily pleased with your journey today.
Pray stay till I've done, and we'll both go together -
For I'm heartily tired of this changeable weather."
But Satan well knew if for Biddy he stayed -
His journey home going would long be delayed,
For Harrogate waters such wonders can do
That the devil himself is oft robbed of his due!"

Holy water is used today in Roman Catholic chapels and households. The water is blessed each year, before the Easter midnight Mass, using the ancient liturgy of the Holy Saturday ceremonies. The water is then placed in holy water stoups, set in the chancel, porches and near small side altars. It is also carried away to fill small stoups in catholic households, that the devout may cross themselves with it, before and after prayers. Holy water is also used at ceremonies such as baptisms, weddings and funerals, and to exorcise evil spirits, lay ghosts and consecrate buildings. The misuse of holy water figures sadly in early witch-hunting records, as, for example, when an unsuspecting black cat, suddenly sprinkled with cold holy water, exploded in blasphemous

At the title page of this chapter we see one of the most fabulous waterfalls in the world at the Yosemite National Park in California, gushing out the sacred waters of Mother Earth herself – Goddess of Goddesses.

On the opposite page is an illustrated symbol of baptism, the origin of which was again not that of Christian dogma, but pagan belief combined with Eastern chakra energy. The beginning was the base energy of the loins in birth and the baptism was a symbolic ritual to transfer this same energy through the body to the head. The dropping of water upon the brow of the child was the conferring of Mother Earth's natural source to allow the higher regions to be connected with the lower. How much we have forgotten!

wrath, and was seriously accused of "demoniacal possession", rather than "reasonable feline expostulation"!

In medieval times, when scientific knowledge was scarce and impregnated with the belief in the supernatural, wells in which the water had a definite mineral content were called medicinal wells. But for water where no natural curative element could be found, the cures had to be attributed to the supernatural. This was the only division possible. Medically, the enforced cleansing of the body and the attitude of mind induced, are capable of making any water holy and blessed, and only the icy coldness of the water and the special providence of the custodians can have prevented many of the most crowded wells from spreading more infection than ever they cured. The laws for lepers, obliging them to drink only from their own bowls, to wash downstream, to keep outside churches and away from all shrines where others worshipped, were sound hygiene. There are however some examples of holy wells that never claimed any medical properties but entirely miraculous ones. St. Winifred's Well (Welsh Gwenfrwddi) in Wales is a holy well that still remains in use after 1,300 years.

LEADING TO THE LEY

But water represents much more than this, for it forms the center of perhaps the oldest and the newest of belief structures. Since the beginning of man's awareness of the divine and the sacred, water has been the essential feature of life. The ancient presence of water filled the Earth with an awareness of divinity and the ancients, especially the Stone Age shamans, gave precedence to the underground water movements as they built temples such as Stonehenge and Avebury, which today have been shown to form the center of many energy meridians.

It wasn't by chance that Stonehenge was erected on the spot it stands on. The calculations of the ancient religions took into

Further monuments to the sources of Mother Earth are the well, page 144, which functioned as a channel for fertility and the complex flows of energy through the ground itself. Glastonbury, on these pages, was where Christianity, and some say Christ himself, arrived in Northern Europe. The place of the tower is the central pivot of the ley lines or "dragon currents", terrestrial energies which connect the entire planet with the rest of existence.

account "scientific" understanding of the earth, the stars and the stones that stood between the two. It is as though the thousands of stone circles scattered across Europe were placed there in combination with the water sub-courses and the ley-lines of energy that criss-crossed the land.

These leys were originally thought, by 19th century investigators, to be simply pathways that had long been used from ancient times and had therefore "engraved" themselves onto the land, even though in most cases these criss-crossings of England, for example, were no longer visible. But more recently they have be shown to lie beneath the surface as meridians of energy rather similar to the meridians of energy in the human body that acupuncturists use as the basis for their cures.

The first man to really propound the theory that there were ancient "tracks" across the countryside was Alfred Watkins, a Hereford brewer and local magistrate. He noticed that churches, mounds, standing stones and other hilltop ancient monuments, were connected by "old straight tracks" other than the obvious

Glastonbury Tor is considered by some to be Holy Grail itself and the focus of Gilgamesh and many of the ancient heroes. The cup was believed to be the spiral labyrinth which encircles the whole cosmic power center at the Tor. The central point of the spiral concentrates the flows of energy and thus protects all those in its influence. Out of this too, came the dragon slayers, for the dragon was the force and the slayer tamed the vortical energy and tapped into it.

ones – the "Green Roads" of the countryside. He called them "leys" or "leas" after a writer named Williams-Freeman who had also pointed out these invisible tracks.

The word "ley" was derived from the fact that many British towns have names which end in "ley" or "leigh," and that this ending originally implied "an enclosed field," so that leys were thought to be enclosures within the areas of such towns. But Watkins made the observation that some of the towns with names ending in ley did not have enclosed fields and that actually, the word was originally only intended to imply that a grassy track existed across the local country.

Perhaps the most exciting revelation of the discovery of these ancient tracks was the understanding that the "one true faith", that of the ancient pagan beliefs, had mapped the entirety of England with a series of lines that brought the whole of the land under a religious mapping. The pattern of the leys was sacred in itself.

The inspired antiquarian Dr. William Stukeley, researching the ancient stone circles during the eighteenth century, wrote in his book on Avebury:

The ancients indeed did make huge temples of immense pillars in colonnades, like a small forest; or vast concaves of cupolas to represent the heavens; they made gigantick colosses to figure out their gods; but to our British Druids was reserv'd the honour of a more extensive idea, and of executing it. They have made plains and hills, valleys, springs and rivers contributing to form a temple of three miles in length. They have stamp'd a whole country with the impress of this sacred character, and that of the most permanent nature. The golden temple of Solomon is vanish'd, the proud structure of the Babylonian Belus, the temple of Diana at Ephesus, that of Vulcan in Egypt, that of the Capitoline Jupiter are perish'd and obliterated, whilst Abury, I dare say, older than any of them, within a very few years ago, in the beginning of this century, was intire; and even now, there are sufficient traces left, whereby to learn a perfect notion of the whole.

LEY-VISIONS

Perhaps one of the most extraordinary aspects of the discovery of these ancient connections between stone circles and earth mounds was that men and women such as Watkins, Stukeley, A.E. (George Russell), Mrs Maltwood, made their discoveries initially through some kind of "hidden vision" – during moments of revelation while contemplating the countryside.

Alfred Watkins, for example, on a hot summer afternoon on

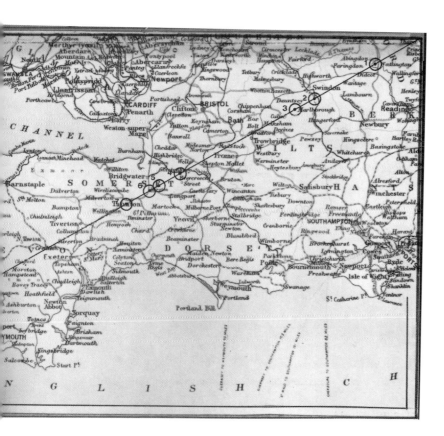

The map on these pages is a typical delineation of the ley lines in England. The dead straight line traces hilltop shrines dedicated to St. Michael or other dragon-killer saints of the past. Running down the "spine" of England it stops, at least as far as the land is concerned, at St. Michael's island rock near Land's End in Cornwall.

It is believed, according to local legends, that this line coincided with the second appearance of Christ on the path between St. Michael's Mount and St. Michael's Tor in Glastonbury.

Ley lines are perhaps our most ancient sacred forms of energy for they drift as "electric" energy formations beneath the ground and somehow also coincide perfectly with underground currents of water. Ley line hunters trace double lines like railway tracks and using dowsing methods, many investigators have found almost inexplicable forms of energy that criss-cross the entire land-mass of Europe and the United States. Races and tribes of the past knew always of these lines, presumably using similar methods to modern dowsers, and invariably built their monuments upon them, usually at the multiple cross-roads of the lines.

the 20th June 1921 was visiting Blackwardine in Herefordshire in England. He stopped on a hilltop to look at his map and then sat and meditated on the view below. In some kind of flashing trance he actually saw something that no one in England had apparently seen for thousands of years. Somehow, perhaps with the same sight as the shamans of the Stone Age, Watkins saw through the surface of the landscape ahead of him down to a layer that had been deposited during a prehistoric age. He saw a web of lines that linked holy places together – stone circles, mounds, crosses and old churches that had been placed on this web by pre-Christian peoples to include even ancient trees, moats, holy wells

On this page is Cirencester Park, a magnificent example of the working of the ley line with local architecture. Eighteenth-century, wealthy land owners created landscapes with long straight pathways that radiated out from the central house. Many of the "straight tracks" were built on ley lines and even though today the aristocracy has lost its influence over the land and the surroundings villages, many of the tracks remain.

linking mountains and hilltops. In that magical moment Watkins had jumped across the whole era of Christian dogma, by-passing the religion that had temporarily drowned the one true faith, and touched the reality of man's sacred divinity inscribed right there in the land itself.

"Then without warning it all happened suddenly. His mind was flooded with a rush of images forming one coherent plan. The scales fell from his eyes and he saw that over many long years of prehistory, all trackways were in straight lines marked out by experts on a sighting system. The whole plan of the Old Straight Track stood suddenly revealed.

His lightning comprehension bore all the marks of being an ancestral memory of the Old Straight Track, just as John Bunyan's ancestral memory of the same thing was at work when he wrote 'The Pilgrim's Progress' and Hilaire Belloc's when he wrote 'The Path to Rome'." (from Allen Watkin's biography of his father).

Alfred Watkins himself described the event: *"I knew the Golden Age was all about me, and it was we who had been blind to it, but that it had never passed away from the world."*

What became most clear to these pioneers of the ancient beliefs was that their revelations were from the unconscious mind – or perhaps from some universal consciousness that had chosen to reveal itself to them.

However, initially, during the early 1900s the explorers of the Old Straight Tracks in England could not make total sense out of the evident existence of something other than ordinary tracks. There was no full understanding of the "invisible" element of leys as far as Watkins and his contemporaries were concerned: they simply connected churches or hilltop sights with one another and their formation was accomplished by Stone Age man in the same way as the modern surveyor does his work – with a sighting stave from a hilltop lined up with another stave at the point of contact. The ley would then have been set between the two. He also

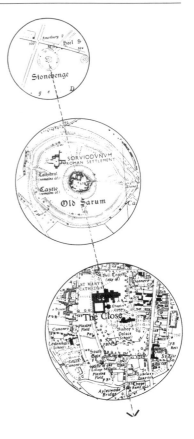

suggested that the Stone Age surveyor would have been accorded special status, similar to a shaman or priest. As a result of Watkins' interest and writing on the subject of leys, a ley-hunting club was formed which reported the findings of the various members and created a momentum for this strange "hobby" resulting in some unexpected findings.

Hunters discovered that leys actually very often came in the form of two parallel tracks instead of simply one, and often, major monuments such as Stonehenge and Old Sarum, Grovelly Castle and others were joined as triangles or squares. In fact, pretty soon, the ley-hunters club found that their new interest was rapidly becoming a very confusing one.

These pages show some more glorious examples of the ley line "in action". The diagrams on this page illustrate the lines between Stonehenge, Old Sarum and the Chapter House of Salisbury Cathedral as they stand in almost perfect alignment. The distance from Stonehenge to Old Sarum is six miles, one hundred times exactly the mean circumference of the Stonehenge lintel ring – 316.8 feet.

Around the same time as the above-ground hunters were finding these confusing results, another man, named Underwood, was investigating the underground aspect of leys. He was interested in establishing how the major monuments of the Stone Age and Celtic periods were connected by water – by streams, or what he called "blind springs" – that ran under the monuments or radiated out from them. But while he was making his experiments, using dowsing rods, he also found that there was another magnetic force beneath the earth which seemed to run at the same level, below the ground in parallel tracks, narrower than the water streams, but definitely joining the monuments in a separate manner to the streams and blind springs. He suggested that the water streams were of "negative" force and the other "tracks", which he named "aquastats," were positive in form. The two did not always run on the same track, but often they did. And where they did run together, they tended to join holy sites together. He therefore named these double sets of underground tracks, "holy lines".

These tracks did not, of course, run in straight lines in the way that Watkins' above-ground tracks did. They criss-crossed each other regularly and moved in circles and loops across the land. They also tended to be the tracks used by animals, picked up through some instinctual connection. But, still more significant was the fact that old roads were aligned to these underground tracks,

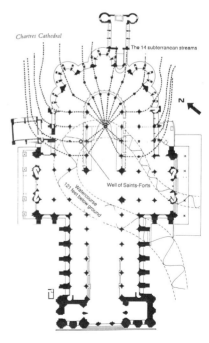

Chartres Cathedral

The 14 subterranean streams

Well of Saints-Forts

Watercourse 121 feet below ground

The map on this page shows the extraordinary discovery of the water course beneath Compostela Cathedral where 14 regular streams converge and are arranged like a fan from beneath the Choir of the Cathedral. It seems almost unbelievable that a simple natural event would conspire with nature to create such a coincidence of energy.

But what is still more extraordinary is the fact that beneath the Choir of the Cathedral of Chartres there are also 14 streams converging! How can nature possible have such knowledge!?

indicating that man was once able to detect them through the same instinct as animals did.

Stonehenge is perhaps one of the most significant of the stone monuments to be connected by the leys that Underwood investigated. He found it to be the center of a huge series of leys, the outer ditch – the earliest built part of the monument – was defined by a great wide loop of energy lines which form a circle that curls back around the Heel Stone.

The famous White Horse of Uffington in England is also almost entirely defined by these ley lines, while the hill named Dragon Hill, which lies under the Horse, has a pair of blind springs

On previous pages we can sample further phenomena of the water courses and ley lines of the English countryside. Mysterious tracks across unlikely parts of the land, small holes in walls that coincide with gates in walls, lintel-capped posts, chalk giants inscribed onto the land at exact points of cosmic energy and stories of ghostly dogs that bound out of entrances and disappear into holes in the walls opposite!

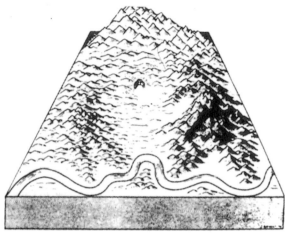

And the story of the ley, or dragon currents does not end in Europe for the Far East can also boast all manner of similar phenomena. On Page 156 is a photograph of the straight line in the Valley of the Thirteen Tombs near Peking. Here, burials are not permitted along the lines for fear of damaging the energy lines of the earth currents beneath.

beneath the chalk marks, and above these springs the grass never grows. The Cerne Abbas giant is also defined by ley lines and it may be that the ancient priests knew of the lines and "drew" the chalk figures to coincide with them.

But the "ley" line does not only exist in Britain. It happens to be of greater interest there simply because there exists a more thorough tradition of interest in leys in England. In China, for example, the equivalent of the ley is called "feng-shui" and the same principle applies: towns, monuments and important centers are erected on the tracks that energize the earth. In Australia, the Aborigines' earliest race memories include a kind of terrestrial nervous system on the land. The Australian natural features of hills, streams, rocks and tracks were traditionally shaped by their ancestors in Dream Time, an endless age that precedes our own and which continues to move in an inaccessible dimension – inaccessible to all except the Aboriginal shaman, who will often use these "tracks" to predict accurately the coming of visitors, storms or other changes in weather conditions. The Hopi Indians also use similar systems of communication.

The whole ley controversy – what are they for, where did they originate, what do they mean – continues without clear answers. But what we can be sure of is that they were "visible" to the ancients as a part of the holy connection between man and nature, man and his planet – the Mother Earth Goddess, with her meridians of power and force was as much alive as any human that occupied her land.

In Australia the sacred life of the Aborigines is centered around the night-time gatherings or "corroberees" such as the one on this page where rituals are associated with earth's powers and the spirits that run in dream time.

Perhaps we will discover in future years, the fact that the entire planet is made up of a plethora of ley lines and dragon currents criss-crossing everywhere and that these currents connect us also to other planetary bodies throughout local and the outer systems of worlds.

How dramatic it would be should we find that Mars, Jupiter and Venus are also possessed of such energy currents and that their power to connect us is similar to the nerve and blood systems of the human body, everything tied together by a cosmic fabric of connections.

On the page opposite we see a picture of a scene in the Sahara Desert where circular formations have been created by natural conditions rather like the burial mounds found all over Europe. It is clear that man and nature once had a lot in common.

Thus the ancient religions based their concern for their greatest
Goddess, Earth, upon her outward manifestations of power and
energy. The water courses and leys were detectable by the human
mind even if they were not visible to the eye, so that there has to
be some significance that we moderns are not now aware of. We
witness their existence but we question their use. Our ever-
constant concern for rational explanation perhaps leads us up the
wrong path. Leys may be associated to irrational explanations.
Irrationality is nothing more, after all, than the presently
unexplained. What is irrational to us was clearly wholly
understandable to our ancient ancestors.

We build our sacred places upon the energy sources of Mother
Earth, that seems sure. But perhaps there is a reverse aspect to this;
perhaps the energy sources and forces of earth grow out of our

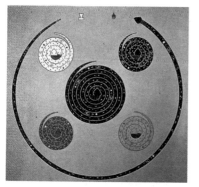

determination to create sacred places. It may be that many of the
ley lines, streams and energy sources arose out of events that took
place in those places. Perhaps Stonehenge was not built on ley
lines, but ley lines occurred around and beneath Stonehenge
because of the intensity of the site's creation. Hundreds, even
thousands of years of devotion and determination in one place
might be enough to change that place and create the sacredness
that we now wish to understand.

THE TALES OF DE-COO-DAH

But we Europeans cannot lay claim to any exclusivity of the ley line. Long before Alfred Watkins had experienced his clairvoyant sight of the underground lines, a man named William Pidgeon had published a book on his discoveries of linear tracks between ancient monuments in the United States.

Pidgeon lived in the early and mid-1800s as an Indian trader traveling throughout the new American continent and had also

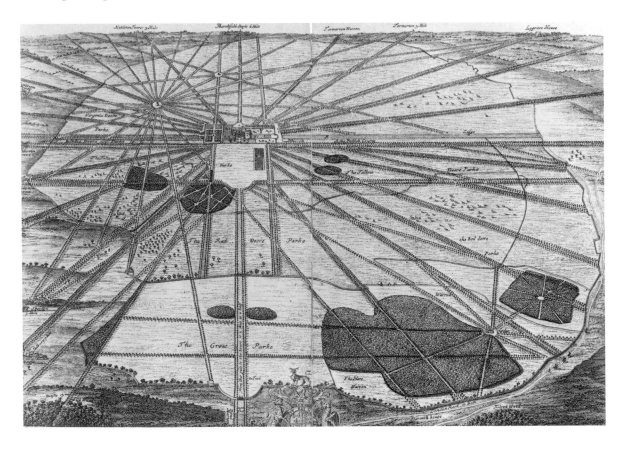

The magnificent illustration opposite depicts the ley landscape at Badminton on the estate of the Duke of Beaufort. The staggering variety of fanned lines that spreads out from the central residence almost gives the impression that the nobility of man could also have been connected with power lines beneath the earth – as though knighthood gave rise to energy and the lines were connected at the base of human power.

owned a store on the Little Miami River in Ohio close to the enigmatic Fort Ancient. In the early part of the 19th century, before the "Christian" community of mankind had wrought almost total devastation on the land, there were thousands of huge earthworks and mounds scattered all over America. Sadly, the damage done by the arrival of this new civilization was far greater than any done in Europe, where some traditions were at least respected. The American Indians, particularly the Hopi, have said that the coming of the "civilized man" is purely a temporary affair and the great land of America will eventually be returned to its true owners. In the same way as the Christian tradition seems like an interloper in the one true faith of our pagan ancestors, it might be that the American people have merely interrupted the passage of the ancient ways, hiding the old mounds under their modern towns – but hiding them very effectively so that it is hard to imagine that anything from the old times of America could ever effectively re-emerge.

Pidgeon set out from Galena on the Mississippi in a boat to explore the monuments along the upper reaches of the river. On this incredible, yet hardly credited journey, he met an Indian shaman named De-Coo-Dah who provided most of the understanding of the symbols behind the arrangement of the ancient mounds. It became clear that the mounds were not placed simply anywhere but were arranged along straight tracks over huge areas of land. They were also almost always close to water, either the river itself or springs, and at the places where the lines intersected one another there was invariably a monument of some kind in the form of animal or human-shaped earthworks.

It seems as though the Indians made their journeys across the vast continent using these straight tracks as references, and although modern archaeologists tend to be sceptical of such ideas it may only be because they have had little or no experience of the way in which the American Indian lived. Alfred Watkins was fascinated by Pidgeon's writings and wrote an account in the *Toronto Star* during the 1920s of how the Indians of Texas move across the land using the monuments and hilltops as map reference.

"You may see an Indian crouch down behind the taller heap, sight over the low one and mark the ferthest object in a straight line, which is likely to be a clump of bushes on the horizon. Then he rides towards those bushes and finds – not water, as he expected, but two other heaps of rocks. Sighting as before, and taking a rockfaced cliff, perhaps towards the south-west, as a goal, he rides a couple of miles farther, and there, trickling out from beneath the cliff's rocky brow, is a spring of fresh, clear water.

It is said that whenever a band of Indians came upon a new spring they built the rock heaps along the trail. At any rate, it appears that these ride signposts lead either to water or places that show traces of a former watercourse."

The labyrinths shown on these pages are those of the Hopi Indians, perhaps the most noble and complete of the American Indian tribes. The Hopis call the labyrinth the "Mother Earth" symbol and liken it to their own underground sanctuaries, the Kivas. It was from here that the Hopi emerged from the preceding world. All the lines and passages within the labyrinth form a universal pattern of the Creator which man must follow through the road of life.

Archaeologists exploring the Southwest of the American continent have discovered incredible prehistoric networks of tracks in the form of actual paved roads running between old settlements. In South America the plethora of "old straight tracks" is even more astonishing, as the ancient Mexican lands show the existence of vast lengths of "roads" that stretch down into the Central American continent. The Spanish missionaries followed these tracks into the

The American continent is probably one of the richest landscapes for energy lines and the potential power of the earth. Perhaps the early years of growth have somewhat shadowed these more subtle aspects of the country due to the need for rapid development and growth to material gain, but this century and the next may well show that the land itself has secrets and mysteries to reveal that will show us something completely unexpected.
The inheritance given to us by the American Indian is just now being listened to, the ancient rituals and stories passed down for generations of wise men and women which the "civilized" American has been ignoring during his brief stay on their land. It may even be that there are greater mysteries to be enjoyed in America than anywhere else in the world.

very ancient sacred places of the native religion which they then, of course, destroyed by enforcing conversion to Christianity. The chapels and crosses put up by these Christian missionaries nevertheless still mark the same spots where the ancient religions had their monuments, so that once again, despite the presence of Christianity, the old ways are still visible.

There is a mountain landscape in Bolivia which, when

Already, archaeologists have discovered prehistoric networks of leys in the southwest of the US continent which still form paved roads running between ancient settlements.

"Roads" stretch up from the South American country into Mexico and the Central American land mass showing the connections between the two ends of what was once one world for nomadic inhabitants. Spanish missionaries followed these tracks and found the many native religious relics on their journeys, sadly often destroying them in favor of the new religion of Christianity, perhaps one of the most destructive forces in the history of the world.

Throughout the world then, these tracks connect and combine from a time when the planet was one, even if much of the different tribes were unaware of one another. The same force combined all the inhabitants of the world, the same natural focus of energy connected everyone.

photographed from the air, displays the most extraordinary pattern of trackways in straight lines, untroubled by any obstacles but linking the sacred places of the Aymara Indians.

The existence of the ley line in America and South America seems to confirm one amazing fact: the concept of sacredness and the connection of monuments, special sites, meeting places, burial

The illustration on this page is of a shield medicine wheel used by American Indian shamans for curing sickness.
Opposite are the ruins of the Pueblo Bonito.

166

The tracks traced upon this landscape, photographed from the air, are from a mountainous region of Bolivia, displaying an astonishing pattern in straight lines, regardless of the many obstacles along the way. The tracks link sacred places of the Aymara Indians.

Opposite bottom of page is the famous "Humming Bird" etching in the stony ground of the Nazca Desert in Peru. This is but one of many designs discovered from the air some half century ago.

Also above is yet another astonishing ground relief of a shepherd and his sheep etched into the earth with numerous circles and designs, once again found in Peru. The American Indian is now receiving perhaps a little more attention in this "New Age" of interest in the sacred but until we can absorb his ancient sources and take part in his rituals, live his life, there is no conceivable way that we can begin to understand what he has left us as an inheritance. It is as strange and incomprehensible as the old magicians. Who understands Merlin or his predecessors? Who then can understand the fathers of America?

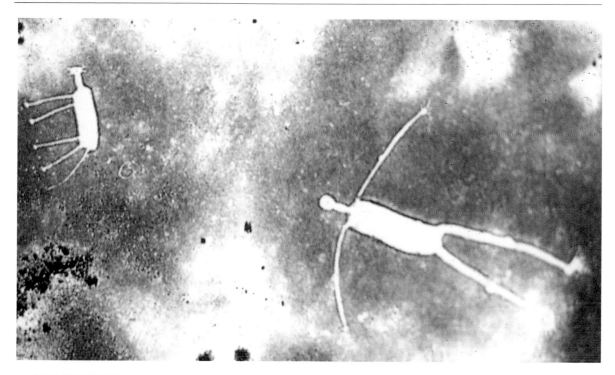

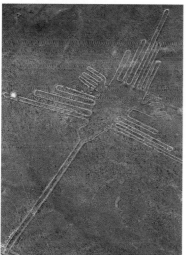

mounds and holy temples was common to all mankind, regardless of their belief structure or understanding of life. The people of the American continent are unlikely to have had any knowledge of the Stone Age people of England or Europe or the Celts or Hindus, and yet they all offered the same system of land coverage, astrological reading and methods of communication. It is clear, even without firm evidence, to anyone with the slightest conscious awareness that the old faith existed with all the people of this planet – a sacredness of the earth itself.

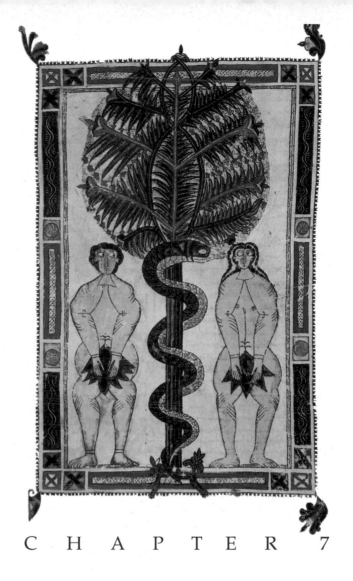

THE
CHRISTIAN BEGINNING

A NEW CULT

Creators of the runes, cravers of war, the Germanic tribes of the Franks, the Vandals, the Visigoths and the Ostrogoths, were the first to move in and finish off the Roman Empire's central axis as it crumbled in the 5th century AD. The Celts had been a fierce and frightening people, but the Germanic tribes were crazy for war. During peace-time, their nobles traveled to other lands to create war just in order to satisfy their needs. Their gods included Woden, the name means "one who makes mad", who was only satisfied by rivers of blood after a battle was fought. Their temples were to the gods that carried on the pagan beliefs and resided in events and needs of the people. But Christianity took too great a hold for these ancient beliefs to survive. By the 7th century AD, the old gods of the Germanic peoples were all but gone and their temples were replaced by churches. They all succumbed to Christianity, except one large group – the Vikings.

The originators of the Christian Cult probably had completely different ideas about their beliefs and the direction of their lives towards divinity than we have had since then. Once Christianity became a world-wide religious force, taken up by the Romans some four hundred years after the death of Christ, its shape and format was molded by unenlightened men with something to gain. No ordinary man can create the uniqueness that came from a Jesus or a Buddha and the result is a bastardized form of belief, packed with dogma and suppression that would probably have made Jesus turn in his grave.

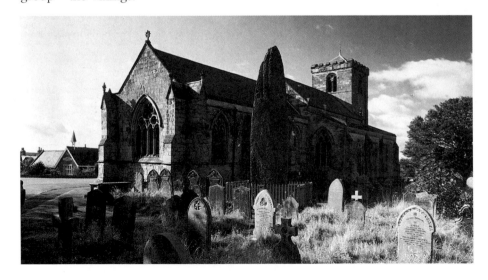

Vikings, Masters of the Pagan Past

Even the Gnostic sects, which still upheld much of the ancient cosmic beliefs at a time when paganism was under its heaviest antagonism from Christianity, with their pure and broadly spiritual interpretation of divinity, came under the hammer. Anything, literally, that gave pause to the Christian dogma, was seen as the work of the devil, a convenient character who, if truth be known, was nothing more than God's senior angel, fallen from grace because he had the courage to stand up against his Master. If God could do so badly as to encompass a potentially evil angel then how can the entire Christian concept of holiness be upheld?

The Vikings might be called the stubborn pagans, for they denied Christianity longer than any other race, although they were exposed to it right up to the 10th and 11th century AD. They came from Sweden, Norway and Denmark and invaded villages and towns as far South as Spain, raping, killing and plundering the Christian churches as though they were the enemy of the world. Perhaps the Vikings were the only ones to realize that the birth of Christianity was, in effect, the death of Mother Earth's reign, the end of the oneness of man with himself and with his world, and the beginning of the one true separative religion, the organized religion that has been the cause of most of mankind's problems in the last two thousand years. At one time, it even looked as though the Vikings might bring Christianity to an end, as they arrived on every European coast in their magnificent long-boats. They even made it to the East Coast of America. The whole of Northern and Eastern England was conquered by them, the Hebrides, Orkneys, Shetlands, Southern Ireland. Hamburg and Paris, Seville and Cadiz were all plundered by the Vikings and the old Gods of the north were reinstated alongside the burgeoning but not yet victorious Christian God. It seemed that no one in Europe had forgotten the pagan Gods and perhaps this time was simply a revival of the old religion, to make man realize that he would never lose their influence.

It has become clear today, in our era of the dying Church, that the old Gods have always been around and that perhaps man only alters the names and retains the essence of the beliefs that were first understood by his most ancient ancestors. Churches in

England, for example, built up to the time of the pestilence in the 14th century, still contained pagan elements, for example a stone phallus inside the altar, and were invariably built on pagan sites, using saints' names that were replacements of the old Gods, arranged very often deliberately so as not to insult the local people.

Today, particularly, there is a fascination with the pagan times. In this New Age, grown perhaps out of dissatisfaction with the organized religions, mankind is turning more towards the old Wicca ways, magic, mysticism, the Eastern philosophies of the self as founder of life.

One of the most mystical and enigmatic devices that has survived from the Viking times are the runes.

The Runes of a Sacred Alphabet

The sacred alphabet of the Norse and Saxons is still a mystery. The modern belief is that the characters that form the magic of each rune were originally Stone Age, found inscribed on rock faces by people in northern Italy. The runes are often found on rock, for example ancient crosses and standing stones or monuments so that it is likely that this theory is accurate. The shape of the symbols is also somehow suitable for rock inscription, so that we may here be dealing with a method of communicating magic that is as old as religious man himself, as ancient as the very first men who understood their true part in existence – the worshipers of Mother Earth herself.

The word rune derives from an Indo-European source – *ru* – meaning secret, and an Old High German word *runer*, which means whisper. We can see from this mysterious derivation that the runes were to be used only by those with special knowledge and the passing down of their secrets was to be done in a whisper.

The carving on this prehistoric axe-like instrument is a symbolic expression of cosmic functions – the universal laws believed to derive from them. These were not fantasies or stories that carried no power. They were directly associated with the focus of the tribal divinity and carried immense force in the hands of those who owned them.

There were also several different runic alphabets – an Old English one, a Gothic one, a Germanic and a Scandinavian one – some having Celtic letters from the Celtic alphabet, known as *Ogham*. Each rune was not simply a letter or sign but was to be combined with a sacred ritual which we have no knowledge of today, so that for each casting of the runes, there was some ritual tribute, understood by the magicians and priests that were entrusted with this task. These people were seen as wizards and formed a special priesthood within the community, wearing animal headdress and deep blue cloaks made of wool. They carried a staff made from hazel or ash wood and wore leather pouches filled with herbs and charms.

As with so many other things, the coming of the Christian Church put an end to the power of the runes, since the priests were persecuted for their pagan and magical beliefs. Still, runic values continued in countries of Europe right through into the 11th century and as late as the 17th century still in Iceland, where presumably the Christian priesthood could not manage to plunder. Even the Lord's Prayer was written in the runic alphabet and used as a magic charm.

And so the old gods and goddesses were gradually subdued under the pressure of the "new" religion of Christ. Much of the ancients still lies within us. The pagan beliefs, born as long ago as seven thousand years or more, are still alive in our old memories in small ways – the tossing of fallen salt, the touching of wood. The Goddess Wyrd and her two sisters, Balder and Freyja, have been kept alive even as recently as in Shakespeare's play *Macbeth* in the form of the three weird witches. Their abode was the Tree of Yggdrasil and here they controlled the fate of human beings by spinning out the thread of life. We touch wood as a tribute to this tree and these three sisters, to protect us against calamity. We may have allowed such acts to become "mere superstition," but the power of them still lies dormant somewhere, perhaps waiting for new life. As man forgets his rational ties to the Christian God, the old pagan feelings may dawn again.

The Christian Celts, converted during the latter part of Celtic history, linked the new religion with old pagan beliefs, undertaking their lives very much still in the psychic connections that paganism had enjoyed for thousands of years. These statues, created by Celtic Christians could well simply be ancient gods of some mysterious tribe were it not for the the crozier and the bell being held by one of them. Perhaps this was some kind of token admission for the benefit of the missionaries that pestered their world for converts!

THE CHRISTIAN CULT

Christianity began life in about the 2nd century AD, simply as a cult, somewhat like those that are around today, like the Theosophists or the Rajneesh people. A small minority of people preaching the word of their "Master" Jesus and his God, "The God". The real change only occurred when the Roman Emperor Constantine adopted the religion as his own and gave it precedence over others with civil rights for the Christian disciples, in the 4th century AD, three hundred years after Jesus had died. It is almost as though Christianity "caught on" purely by luck and good publicity. It was nothing more than the adherence of a few people to a relatively unknown God, like many of the others such as Bacchus or Lug, and then, because of the "loud voice" and interest of a man of influence, the cult began to develop and grew into something which we can now view in the form of such institutions as the Vatican, with all its beauty and power on one side and its evident deterioration on the other. It is as though the original Christian cult has run its course, a merely temporary organization of man's beliefs that actually grew from the same routes as the original religiousness of mankind, set in the Earth herself.

Much of the Christian dogma was familiar to the people of the time of Constantine in Western Europe – belief in the virgin birth, the son who was also the father, and the resurrection. These were all themes of the ancient fertility religions. The priest, Jesus Christ,

Ritual and belief throughout the history of man, has always been handed down by one father or mother to the next child, the traditions to be continued and the religions to be nurtured. This has been so in all lands – for the aborigines, the American Indians, the Celts and Hindus. It is only because of a gap in our willingness to listen that such stories have ceased to be of importance and that gap was brought about by the forceful and determined Christian focus which gave no energy to the dangerous and dominating paganism.

who also performed the sacrifice on the cross, dying for the lives of the people, and whose body and blood were converted for the followers into bread and wine during worship, were entirely familiar since the times of the earliest religious man. There was nothing new here and the people who adopted the Christian beliefs did nothing more than adapt their own deeper understanding to the new "fashion".

But very often the adaptation was not so easy, for the missionaries of this new Christianity were forceful and adamant about their beliefs and conversion was often not a gentle matter. Churches were built on the sites of pagan monuments and ancient rituals were discouraged actively, though mostly to no avail. The people tended often only to give lip service to Christianity and continue in their original and much longer lived beliefs.

Jesus Christ, the man behind the belief, was little known for hundreds of years. Stories and legends about him increased as time went on, but, to begin with, no one much knew who he was and what his purpose might have been. It is almost as though the Christian God has grown only out of man's imagination and love of embellishment, adapted for an earthly people who knew better but accepted for fear of troubles if they did not.

In 325 AD Jesus of Nazareth was deified by the Nicene Council – a man-made council of course, naming once again its own gods. One hundred years after this Mary was named "Mother of God", her deification taking place once again through purely political methods: the Patriarch Cyril gathered a large group of supporters together in one council, and managed to persuade those present that she was not only human but the new version of the Mother Goddess, thus creating the basis for Christianity's cult of Mary, "kept free from all stain of original sin" – though today it is not clear how sin can ever be original or stained. Perhaps the only original sin is that of the concept of purity, the Christian idea of suppression which has done so much damage to mankind's freedom and understanding of sexuality.

Mary, Mother of God

The biggest problem for the newly established Church was that Mary herself broke one of the first rules – she was both Mother of God and Bride of God – so that these patriarchs of purity had do go through various complex and theological hoops in order to put the situation in an intellectual light worthy of the pure religion that so much discouraged the pleasures of the flesh. The Christian concept of celibacy within the priesthood undoubtedly derived from the ancient cult of the Virgin, but, like many Christian substances, the new purity bastardized the old beauty. The Virgin was originally a woman of power -- her virginity an abstinence which was attributable to the deity and gave strength through continence. It was magical rather than ethical. The new celibacy turned something of incredible religiousness into something crude and dirty, resulting in today's heavy problems within the modern priesthood where celibacy has done no more than lead to homosexual practices, venereal disease, AIDS and perversion within the Church.

Even more imaginative in its hoop-jumping was the method by which Mary managed to acquire the fetus of Jesus without committing the awesome sin of enjoying the act. Jesus was, after all, a partly human creature and therefore presumably born out of human substance – spermatozoa. Where did this very sexual seed derive from? Theologians, in their determination to remain ignorant of the true method of conception, persuaded some that Mary received the seed from the Holy Ghost, presumably not substantial enough to penetrate her in the normal way, achieving the result by depositing it in her ear! As though he had aimed and somehow missed! This wide shot was not in fact so far off the mark in terms of the understanding of the time, for in the 12th century conception was not understood at all, the belief being that the man deposited the completed fetus into the woman's body. Patriarchy, of course, could not concede that the woman had anything to do with the formulation of the child's body. Women were, after all, mere vessels without importance in matters of procreation, or anything else for that matter, particularly as there was not even supposed to be any pleasure in sexual union. The creation of a new life had to be done by the man. The priesthood took the matter a stage further, stating that the fetus was stuck inside Mary's ear.

Even illustrations were drawn to show the process to a largely illiterate people, a picture of Mary standing with a shaft running down from God in heaven into her ear. The Mary statues in the Churches sometimes even had a little door at the back and inside a cavity within the wooden edifice would be a small, already formed child.

With this growing "singular" religion – only one family to rely upon – Christianity gave succor by producing its many saints. At least if God or Jesus or Mary didn't work out, you could turn to one of the many saints instead. From this point of view, there wasn't really so much difference from the old religions – just a few changes of names – different positions in the game of mystical chairs. But the real difference arose out of the proximity of the divine. In the ancients' way of looking upon perfection, the divine lived right here on earth, there was no distance between humanity and that which it worshipped. With the new Christian belief systems the divine was "out there" in heaven – far away, beyond all reach and only to be attained by impossible determination, thus giving the priesthood a constant hold on the individual who could never manage to attain holiness. God had gone so far away that no one could ever hope to reach him.

The rock, in all its forms, such as bearer of cross or part of a circle, was the knowledge of earth. It was also the central power of the land. In the inception of electric power, so the essence of the natural forces have been lost.

MERCVRIVS 1984

THE RISE
AND FALL
OF WICCA

One of the other major aspects of the new Christianity was its
denigration of women. As we saw in the chapter on the Celts, in
the old religions women were accorded equal standing with men,
both in battle and priesthood – seemingly a natural state for them.
But in the Christian ethos, sex was an abhorrence. It may seem, or
begin to seem a very strange state of affairs that the basic essence
of humanity – its sexual energy – could be regarded as "unnatural,"
but the fundamental attitude of the Christian Fathers was that
women were degrading…little better than whorish creatures who
tempted men away from their holiness! The standing of
womanhood therefore fell steeply. Women during menstruation or

But it is not over yet! The ancients have remained underground, beneath the modern organized religions, waiting patiently to arise again to the surface and we begin to see this most forcefully in the very recent past. The Human Potential Movement, the new "Wicca" beliefs, the modern gurus, all bring mankind back in touch with a more honest proposal of life and divinity.

But all such proposals are entirely based upon the pagan past. There is nothing new about the May Day Celebrations that take place in many parts of America each year. They are as they were three thousand years ago, only the people have changed. Some would say not even them, for they are simply spirits returning to other bodies – and it is the spirits that carry the ultimate memories.

after childbirth were not permitted inside Christian churches, presumably because of some mixture of superstition, i.e. the old paganism, and the idea that women were spiritually inferior to men.

The overriding stupidity of the patriarchal rulers fostered the witch hunts throughout Europe, though the ancient Wicca religion was still alive beneath the surface, with its own priesthood, largely watched over by women who understood and continued to practice the rites of Mother Earth, the old understanding that God lived inside life, not outside it. This subterranean belief that nature was divine and connecting all life with her vitality remained throughout Christianity as a second religion and is still alive, perhaps today, preparing to resume its original force during the next millennium. Essentially, the old religion has remained alive through the need of mankind to live off his planet. A God who only insists on moral attitudes does not provide dinner!

Unfortunately it can now be seen in retrospect that much of the anxiety and bloodshed produced by the Christian Church was brought about by the denial of nature and the insistence on false values of holiness. The result is visible today, for we have largely lost the love and appreciation of our land and our planet. We are apparently happy to destroy it in the name of "progress" because we do not see that it sustains us in the name of its own godliness. Much of this attitude can be laid at the door of Christianity.

But somewhere within the darker and more romantic recesses of Christianity lay more attractive aspects. So much of the life of Jesus and his God, the Father, was a continuation of the same stories that were familiar to the Celts. This was a powerful religion with unusual powers. The continued rituals of the Christian Church were not so far from the old ways – the number three, the Trinity, the new translation of the same gods – and this persuaded the greater part of Europe to accept and adopt the new and potentially great religion.

C H A P T E R 8

CRYPTIC
KARMA

CRYSTALIZING THE ANCIENTS

Just forty years ago, at the end of World War Two, very little of this book, and certainly this chapter, would have made any sense or have had any appeal to the majority of people. It is only since the late 60s that an interest in the ancient religions has once again come to life in a wider field. And particularly in the last decade, the 80s, this interest has blossomed, largely because of the existence of two factors – a disillusionment with many forms of 20th century life, and the experience of certain individuals who have somehow crystallized the ancient paths into modern methods. In this chapter we will look at the origins of some of the new religious forms, the sacred places that they derive their power from and the new sacredness that is developing out of the changing religious world that we are entering. We will look at one of the strongest foundations of this new form of religious sacredness, Buddhism, and then at the people that have surrounded the modern Masters, who have today set up their own sacred places in the form of modern ashrams.

In this century, especially during the last fifty years since the Second World War, there have been more "international shamans" than in many centuries.

The Buddhist Foundation

Krishnamurti, Rajneesh, Da Free John, Gurdjieff, and many others, have arisen from the crowd and caused all manner of major changes to our beliefs and established understandings of life and religion. It is as though they come at an opportune time, all in an army of change

For the first time, these Masters have made a major impact on western thought. In the past, the more significant religious leaders of the East remained influential largely in the East and western people had only a minority interest in their activities. This century we have seen not only Eastern religious leaders such as Rajneesh and Krishnamurti, create major followings in the western civilized countries, but we have also seen western gurus emerge. Men such as Gurdjieff and Da Free John have grown to the heights of enlightened understanding from a western conditioning.

Nobody knows exactly when the man who was to become Buddha was born. As far as history can be sure the date was around 563 BC in Lumbini, a village in what is now southern Nepal, right next to the Indian border. He died in 483 BC and to put some measure to his position in history, Socrates was six years old at Buddha's death, so that the Master of Masters was not in our history so very long ago.

His name was Siddhartha Gautama and his father was the leader of a people known as the Shakyas, which explains the other name given to Buddha, Shakyamuni, "Sage of the Shakyas". The name Buddha means "Awakened One," or "Enlightened One." Essentially, therefore Buddha was a strange mixture: a chieftain of a "royal" family, a warrior caste member and a man of extraordinarily un-warlike character. His development into the state of enlightenment followed a personal determination to abandon great wealth and simple family contentment in favor of a life that would be devoted to the improvement of mankind's desperate state of suffering.

Leaving his royal state and his wife and family, he donned the

The Enigma of Enlightenment

yellow robes of the Indian pilgrim and embarked on a spiritual quest. Fairly soon he abandoned the orthodox religious attitudes and entered a period of extreme deprivation and asceticism, in order to test this aspect of his own spiritual growth, eventually concluding that it was not of any value and abandoning the ascetic life, propounding to others that they should do the same. Adopting therefore a middle way between the riches that he knew and the poverty that he had experienced, the Buddha-to-be achieved enlightenment beneath a tree at a place now named "Bodh Gaya", some fifty miles south of the River Ganges.

This is, of course, a brief account of his life up the point at which he was transformed from a normal man into an enlightened being. Modern understanding or at least accounts of the understanding of the process of enlightenment show that the whole physical and mental breakdown which takes place in order for a man or woman to be able to find this "altered" state of being, requires enormous and powerful strength and determination. Those that have undertaken this journey in similar ways to the Buddha recount extraordinary suffering and physical stress followed by major experiences, which appear to be related to nothing short of a physical death where the body literally ceases to operate in the normal way. If Gautama the Buddha underwent this form of human metamorphosis then he was himself a walking sacred place and his force and subsequent intelligence would have been powerful enough to command a world religion of extraordinary proportions, at least as powerful as Christianity and perhaps longer lived.

The Buddha's enlightenment is in fact the central feature of the Buddhist religion – as important a basis as the Crucifixion is to Christianity – and in fact, much of the New Age vision of religion that is coming to life today is also based on the enlightenment of those who now call themselves or are called by others, Masters.

The Buddha had reached a state which can only be described as a state in which one "understands" reality – he was evidently, and without personal doubt, in touch with clear and simple

Somehow we can accept the presence of a Buddha or a Jesus Christ for we have had a long history of conditioned belief in respect to these names. There is no human presence, only a distant and magnificent godliness that we have never experienced directly. But when a living Master appears, a man who displays all aspects of enlightenment, all inspirational qualities of one that has a direct connection with divinity, we miss him. We could not see a second Jesus if he was standing before us because our own habits deny it.

Only after death, and probably after a long period of time, do we agree to stop being afraid of individuality and become inspired by it.

Perhaps in two or three hundred years from now we will be worshiping, as these Tibetan Buddhist monks above, at the temple of Osho Rajneesh, the man so much hated by America following his problems with the Reagan administration. Perhaps we will need new religions in the future, once the glitter of the Christian Church has finally faded and left our sight clearer again.

knowledge of how life works. His additional gift was that, both before and after his enlightenment took place, he was an extremely charismatic person and this, too, is a feature of the great Masters of our past and present. Whether it is the process of enlightenment which produces the charisma, or whether enlightenment comes to those who possess a high degree of human potential, is hard to say. Probably the two go hand-in-hand. The majority of human beings have neither clarity/enlightenment nor charisma, so that it is not surprising that such men as Buddha and others that have lived since him, some also alive today, attract us to follow them. We see that they have something that we do not and we yearn to know more about it. This is ultimately the whole foundation of sacredness – our worship of those who have the divine within them. We erect thousands of monuments to them and spend thousands of years kneeling to their memory.

The chief place of pilgrimage for the follower of Buddha is Bodh Gaya – a 12th century Mahabodhi Temple placed on the site of the Buddha's enlightenment, the holiest shrine in the Buddhist world.

The Buddha, after meditating for some ten days at Bodh Gaya, went to Sarnath, which lies a few miles from the city of Varanasi on the banks of the River Ganges. Here he preached to the people and his first disciples became monks, or bhikkhu, and the Buddhist religion was born. Sarnath is one of the next most holy places for the Buddhist follower, still today a beautiful and tranquil town. One of perhaps the most strange and unusual places to visit here is the Dhamekh stupa in the Deer Park, an example of distinctive Buddhist architecture, and of course there are many extremely beautiful statues and stone replicas of the Buddha himself.

And naturally the other major event of his story was his death. Where he died there is now a temple, in Kusinara, northern India, where it it still possible to feel the environment, the ground and the feeling of sacredness that has hardly changed since the Buddha died.

GROUNDS FOR BELIEF

Buddhism spread across the world at a tremendous pace with the construction of hundreds of thousands of monuments in Thailand, Japan, Burma, Sri Lanka and many other places. The beauty and sanctity of these monuments to this one enlightened man almost always reflect that sense of peace that he portrayed during his life, and in general the Buddhist religion has produced far less discomfort from within the religion than Christianity did, for it somehow does not seek to conquer or create vast riches for itself, but remains a humble and enlightened belief system. It has, however, been strong enough to cause outside friction and today it

Amongst the temples of the Far East, there is Borobudur in Java, one of the most ornamentally rich creations of the Buddhist faith. It was built in the image of a world mountain, its levels representing ascending stages from earth to the transcendent levels of divinity.

If we look closely at the lower levels of the sculptured stone we see all the pleasures and concerns of ordinary life, and then rising to the higher levels we are given the life of the Buddha Shakyamuni, who taught his disciples a method of release from the unending cycle of rebirth. Still higher we see the young seeker speaking with many teachers in search for his own illumination and then higher the biographical representation of the Buddhist sage Asanga. And at the summit are three Buddhas meditating to show the disciple where the spirit lies – within each of us.

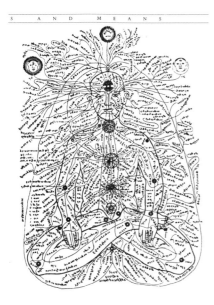

S A N D   M E A N S

This Samadhi completes the transformation and fulfills the purpose of evolution. Now the process by which evolution unfolds through time is understood. This is Enlightenment.
Patanjali.

This simple and calming confirmation was stated by Patanjali two thousand five hundred years ago. Just to read it is to get it! It is also a reminder of what we have subdued beneath the patterns of scientific investigation.

stands against some of its worst enemies – those who see the world as a place for commercial growth and deny the importance of spiritual understanding. The Tibetans struggle to stand up against the advancing madness of the Chinese authorities who would wipe out the race completely and use the country to house their growing hoards, careless of anything but industrial growth. The original Buddhist people, therefore, find themselves today under fire, but Buddhism has also spread across the globe to the Western world and become a stronghold of belief amongst a growing minority who, like so many others, have had their fill of Christian dogma. Jung's famous quote about Zen sums up perhaps the appeal of Buddhism to people who have long lived under the shadow of religious suppression: *"Preoccupation with the riddles of Zen may perhaps stiffen the spine of the faint-hearted European, or provide a pair of spectacles for his shortsightedness."*

The number of people in the West who would claim to be genuine Buddhists is probably not so great yet, though numbers in the United States grow every year. What is far stronger is the number of people concerned with various new religious understandings which in some way derive from Buddhism. Many of the modern followers of present-day gurus derive their belief systems and their new life realizations from doctrines similar to that of Buddha. Their Masters are seen to be enlightened men or women and the structures of the changes that have taken place within them, in order that they might sample enlightenment even second-hand, are similar to those experienced by disciples and monks in the Eastern tradition. It is as though, finally, the East is coming to the West, bringing with it some relief from the madness of progress and the suppression of Christianity.

Some extraordinary temples already exist to these new religions, most of them found in the East still, though there are numerous small centers scattered throughout Europe and the United States. Perhaps these, or some of them, will form the sacred places of the future. It is worth a glancing mention of one of the most impressive of these places.

THE
OSHO
ASHRAM

On the tranquil edge of the astonishingly industrial town of Poona in India lies a small but highly energetic ashram, once named Rajneeshdham, the Indian center of the well known and at one time even notorious religious Master Bhagwan Shree Rajneesh, now named simply Osho.

In a vast residential parkland named Koregaon Park, an area of

Far away from the chatter of gossip, stands a gate which allows anyone entrance to a new sacred place in India, new in the sense of being only begun some three decades ago. This ashram now contains some several thousand visitors each year and a unique atmosphere of the seekers who enjoy its Buddhafield. On January 19th 1990, Osho Rajneesh left his body inside these gates and left behind a stronger sense of divinity than any of the Masters who have survived human behavior this century.

For those who wish to experience such truth, the story continues and lives. For those who wish to find sacredness there is more here than almost anywhere else in the world.

Poona largely inhabited by wealthy Indian families, lies a different world – one that can hardly be compared with anywhere else in India or even the rest of this frantic globe. The air in Poona is so polluted that it is almost impossible to walk the streets without coughing or becoming ill from the floating dust – dust made up largely of cow excrement! But if the visitor leaves the streets and enters this strange and unexpected ashram, the taste of the dust in the mouth disappears, the air is clean and the general sense of anxiety and stress that exists elsewhere, almost instantly vanishes.

The ashram has been here for almost twenty years, occupied during that time, except for five years when he was in America, by the Master Osho and some three thousand or so visiting disciples who come largely from the West and stay short periods, many of them simply to take a break from the increasing horror story of Western "civilized" living. Others spend longer there, entering more seriously the complex and sacred journey of spiritual growth.

The first step, even before being able to walk inside the large ornately designed gates, is to have an AIDS test. The ashram professes to be an AIDS-free zone and, in fact, Osho (Rajneesh) was one of the very first to warn the world against the coming threat of AIDS, instructing his disciples to undertake the precautions which have now been adopted on a world-wide scale. Beyond the entrance is a plant-filled, waterfall atmosphere of soft calm that quickly enwraps the visitor, though there is also an intense sense of order and cleanliness, as though the process of inner understanding were accompanied by the organization of the physical nature of life. Various gardens surround the central area and to one side is the "Buddha Hall," where the formal meditations take place, starting in the early morning with the "Dynamic"

There is some evidence to show that the presence of a gathering of meditators in one place on the planet creates an energy form that then circles the planet and changes its total feeling. It is likely that 99% of those living around the world notice nothing, but there is also a strong likelihood that this sacred energy affects us nevertheless, unconsciously.

When war occurs or major crimes, we all hear about it. We all feel the indignity of negative activities, and equally the activities of a few single hearted individuals in the process of meditation touches our hearts and improves the planet's condition.

meditation, one of Osho's hallmarks in which the body is variously and vigorously shaken, and moving through the day with dance, Sufi and numerous other singing and dancing sessions that can happily occupy the visitor without need for any other activity! The Buddha Hall was also the place where Osho would sit with his people or give discourse.

Other activities nevertheless exist, for behind the front entrance is a larger area inside the main ashram which is fully occupied with therapy sessions, both group and individual. There are opportunities to shed all manner of complex and painful conditionings – characteristics that perhaps we have clung to most of our lives, given to us by our dear parents and the society we so careful protect, but often the cause of intense agony and discomfort.

The extraordinary aspect of this ashram is its power of instant sacredness. For the purposes of this book it illustrates with great precision the very essence of what creates a sacred place. First there is clearly the "business" of spiritual learning happening inside this "temple" – spiritual learning in the sense of inward-looking activities. The circle of the ashram does not primarily concern itself with the outside world, except insofar as it solves or helps to understand the inner mechanisms and their connection with outside activities. Second, there is present the essence of an

It would be foolish then to deny the presence of any ashram or gathering of disciples, however uncertain we may be of their motivations. Past experiences such as those of Jonestown may give us a jaundiced sense about Eastern philosophers but one bad coin does not destroy the potential of a whole treasure. The biggest threat though, of any religious group such as those that Osho Rajneesh gathered around him, was not the likelihood of any mass suicide, but the danger that such disciplehood brings to the order of society – the imposed structure that the patriarchal system has given us.

enlightened Master. Since he left his body on January 19th, 1990, it seems almost as though his atmosphere has grown stronger. The story is told that when Buddha himself died his essence remained within the area of his life for five hundred years thereafter, and Osho's people have, since their Master departed, increased the energy of making their ashram a sacred center.

Osho is not an easy person to define. The daily gatherings inside Buddha Hall which he attended (now still carried on without his physical presence, usually with between two and five thousand disciples present, in silence or watching a video of Osho) were intensely holy affairs with a degree of respect and mutual

One of the major problems that any Westerner faces when becoming involved, even on the periphery of spiritual investigation, is that of "understanding" meditation itself. The problem is that meditation defies understanding of any kind and we have been so much indoctrinated into the precious nature of the mind that we attempt to apply its techniques to everything and the first thing we find when doing this with the subtlety of meditation is that it lies in direct opposition to it.

The very essence of meditative behavior is that the mind becomes absent. During any "successful" meditation the adept loses touch with the normal thought process. Thoughts do not stop coming, for there is little we can do about the chattering of the brain's mechanism, but the passing considerations cease to be of any importance. In effect we watch from another place.

consideration that is unlikely to be found in many other places on this earth. The arrival of the Master himself was an extraordinary experience for those who were at all open to it, for he came in a large Rolls Royce and dressed in the finest robes, a small man but towering in his presence. There is plenty of opportunity for those who cannot grasp the significance of sacred life forms to criticize this man, but strangely, when one remains present in his ashram and when one enjoys the simple activities of his happy and joyous people, all the superficial judgments vanish rather quickly and the main concern is to drink the sacred element of this extraordinary man in this extraordinary place.

The Sediment of Meditation

Thirdly, from the sacred point of view, the ashram contains a large number of people with "like-mind". The sediment of sacred attitudes is laid down by those who occupy the sacred place. All those who live in or visit the Osho ashram propose to alter their personal inner behavior, in order that the world might alter its general condition. This is ultimately the way in which life will improve.

Osho and several other enlightened Masters have stated that it requires only a few hundred disciples meditating together in a condition of calm within themselves, for the force that surrounds this planet to change. It requires only a few areas of intensely active sacred feeling for life on Earth to improve. One of these sacred centers is undoubtedly the Osho ashram in Poona.

SACRED BODY

The concept of karma encompasses many interpretations. There is what we might call "lazy karma," in which the exponent drifts into a state of inaction for fear of creating any situation which may, in a future life, result in problems or burdens. Even the killing of an insect by accident may, of course, result in problems later, for the insect may come back in a future life as your boss! This form of karma has probably done much to create the inactive and often lethargic nature of the Indian nation today.

On the other hand there is a more intelligent attitude that could be applied to the concept of karma which in effect perhaps would result in the sacredness of that body. If we believe ourselves to be "one-life" beings – i.e. we come to the body, we live one life and we die and that's it – then sacredness is a thing of simple superstition and no more. If, on the other hand, we believe that there is a continuous growing power within the human frame – the soul, we might call it – then perhaps through many lives of experience and learning we become sacred ourselves and karma is simply the growth of the sacrosanct soul. In this sense then we are all walking sacred places.

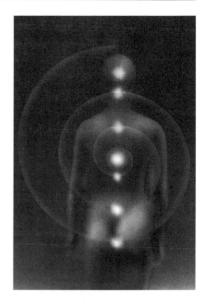

The illustration above is taken from a book published in America in 1988 called *Unknown Man* by an author named Yatri. His proposal of a new kind of individual with physiological changes in the genetic structure coincides with an age-old message that the species of man will alter during this next few generations. That the body will develop new techniques and abilities, including a greater facility with meditative activities.

The illustrations defines the chakra levels and the circular motions of energy that surround and permeate the body. The simple concept here shown is that there are growth levels that rise from the base chakra at the genital area to the brain and once this channel of energy is freed up the body becomes a temple in itself, the mind able to rest and a freedom from anxiety brings an ability which is currently beyond most of us.

Perhaps this is the fate of mankind to come.

C H A P T E R   9

THE
SILENT TEMPLE

T he longing for a sense, an experience, of the divine has always haunted mankind, even driven men mad, for its essence seems wholly in contrast with the social mores of "ordinary" life. If we imagine that our global conditioning was set in motion by the earliest of religious peoples, perhaps Stone Age man or even earlier, people who wandered and lived alone a great deal, always in touch with a natural individuality and very earthly divinity, we can see why, in the deepest part of our race memory we still seek out the silent places in which we can meditate in complete solitude. This is what our ancestors did and this is what all ages of man have tried to do. It is only now that we must

THE ALONE

struggle to find physical space for silence, and perhaps the inner space is the only space that remains untouched.

The early Christian "Fathers" who traveled to Brittany and Ireland, ascetic monks whose task it was to convert the pagan peoples – also carried news of strange "Desert Fathers" who lived as hermits in Egyptian, Arab and Palestine caves during the 4th century. These men were almost like pioneers, for they had their own idea of their relationship with the Christian God – a strictly spiritual relationship which was not given them by some dogma or book. They were alone in their search and uninterested in any organized religion. This was Jesus's original message, which was later ruined by the Church and by mankind's desire to be told what to do.

Such an idea was also deeply felt by the Celts who journeyed on long pilgrimages in search of the divine within silence and aloneness. Their own temperament had always included a desire for solitude and between the 5th and 9th centuries, as though taking the Desert Fathers' example, the western lands were full of wandering hermits seeking places of meditation and silent worship. They traveled far north to the Hebrides and Orkneys islands where the sound of birds and water helped their meditation and where they were also as far away from the established Church as they could be.

The coasts of Wales, Brittany and parts of Spain are peppered with tiny temples sunk into the rock face, with sometimes treacherous pathways like goat tracks leading to remote caves where these hermits lived. In some parts they were designated as saints by the Church, but this would have occurred only after their death, perhaps several hundred years after. The original character, the hermit, sometimes man, sometimes woman, would have lived entirely alone with goats or sheep for company and food, on an inner search that began when he or she found the remote location. It is likely that these hermits did not simply wander in search of just any place but were directed by some past tradition or legend concerning a certain area, perhaps derived from Celtic lore or even

Below we see a silent meditator contemplating the raked gravel of the famous Zen garden in Daisen-in, at the Rinzai Zen Monastery of Daitokuji in Kyoto.
And opposite a natural space for silence and contemplation lies stretched out before the boatman.

Mountain scenes are traditionally places where silence and peace can be achieved. Away from the madness and thought patterns of cities we can take it easy! During the investigations into the differences between city scapes and country areas it has been shown that because of the very nature of anxiety present within a city, those that inhabit these areas are more prone to the same energies. It is harder to be at peace within a city because nobody else is at peace.

early tradition. The ascetic conditions of their lives would very likely often lead to religious, "satori" experiences, to visions and insights which in some cases would also have led to local interest in their presence and thus to stories and eventually perhaps to sainthood, the result probably having little or nothing to do with the original experience. But the Church was always only too eager to capitalize on personal divinity, calling it into place as part of the organized nonsense.

The wandering hermits believed in the presence of God in everything, here and now and not in a future or far-off place. They felt divinity within the birds and animals around them and made a connection, perhaps, with their surroundings as strongly or as intimately as the ancients had done millennia before them. There are all manner of stories about these enigmatic and spiritually rich individuals who lived surrounded by the decay in understanding brought about by the growing power of Christian dogma. They

were said to attract fish and animals to their presence during the private masses they would conduct in the fields or beside rivers. A certain St. Claran had his home built by a local wild boar who constructed a room of twigs and grass for him and then brought a fox, a badger and a wolf to join the hermit's small gathering of animal disciples. St. Cainneck enjoyed a helpful stag's antlers to read his book from and each time St. Molaisse wanted to write, a bird would bring him a feather.

By about the 7th century AD the Celtic people and the Christian Church began to come to some agreement and in the 8th century the Vikings were already invading Europe, making the lives of the wandering hermits impossible. There was to be no silence or meditation for them now and their disappearance also took what was left of the elegance and nobility of the Christian culture in the West. Thus began the disaster of the organized Christian Church which we are still tolerating today.

A meditator takes advantage of the very special energy and atmosphere of a landscape that encourages our more subtle body to elevate to the surface.

On this page we see Edward S.Curtis' picture of the Apache by the Pool. *It's a different kind of world to grow up in when you're out in the forest with the little chipmunks and the great owls. All these things are around you as presences, representing forces and powers and magical possibilities of life that are not yours and yet are all part of life, and that opens it out to you. Then you find it echoing in yourself, because you are nature.*

If you follow your bliss, you put yourself on a kind of track that has been there all the while, waiting for you, and the life that you ought to be living is the one you are living. Wherever you are – if you are following your bliss, you are enjoying that refreshment, that life within you, all the time.

Wherever we go, we may find that bliss, even in the city itself. But there are parts of the world where beauty and tranquillity simply make it easier for those who cannot normally discover their center and their ideal nature.

MYSTICS AND MEANING

In the early Christian Church, before the establishment destroyed individualism, there were some extraordinary mystics who, it must be said, followed a path that was closer to the ancient Greek way than to the new Christian. Their desire was to understand in depth the nature of divinity and in this private and lonely quest they mostly lived in the ascetic tradition of mystics of all time – poor, without possessions and wandering from place to place. They, like the Celts and the ancient religions before them, once again believed in the oneness of existence, the imminence of all things and the presence of God in everything around them. This feature of so many religions and most of the Masters and gurus of past and present is echoed throughout the beliefs of the "silent wanderers" and hermits. Only in the Christian Church did it become denied in the West. The world was not brought into being by a "maker" who lived somewhere "above" – a maker who was responsible for everything, for they knew this to mean a loss of responsibility and love. Instead they understood life to be vital and dynamic – a "becoming" world, that never ceased to change, with a binding force called love.

The essence of aloneness was once again present. The journey for the Christian mystics was one "from the alone to the Alone", the individual, rediscovering the way back to the perfect "World Soul" which was the connector between the timeless divinity and the physical universe.

The Christian mystics knew of Jesus but considered him little more than an historical figure who had become perhaps enlightened as an individual but who represented no more than a great guru of the past. For, as seekers of truth, they longed for living enlightenment, often their own, and if we read writers such as Plotinus and Dionysius, believed to be a Desert Father, we can

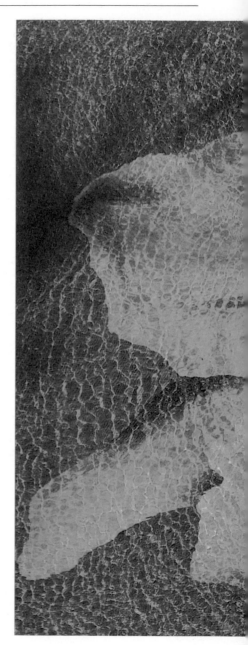

This extraordinary picture taken in a Hawaiian Summer, the man floating aimlessly in water, is another example of the sacred nature that man can find in his surroundings.
We all look for this, some more successfully than others. It might even be that the annual vacation is a search for tranquillity, gradually, sadly these years, being eroded by the increasing presence of development and the madness of the search for personal fortune.

often find far greater beauty and depth than anything found in the words of Jesus Christ. The following passage is Dionysius's portrait of the qualities inherent in silence:

"For the higher we soar in contemplation the more limited become our expressions of that which is purely intelligible; even as now, when plunging into the Darkness which is above the intellect, we pass not merely into brevity of speech, but even into absolute silence, of thought as well as of words. At last, the "entire ascent being accomplished" we become wholly voiceless, inasmuch as we are absorbed in Him who is totally ineffable."

Once again we return to the source of sacredness – this same story repeating itself throughout the background to all other activities and ever present, even today where the civilized world and science have attempted to destroy the beauty of life with no greater strength than labels. We can find the exact same sentiments as those of Dionysius expressed by one who has only recently left the world:

"Learn silence. Here, sit in silence sometimes. Don't go on gossiping, don't go on talking. Stop talking and not only on the outside – stop the inner talk. Be in an interval. Just sit there, doing nothing, just being presences to each other. And soon you will start finding a new way to communicate. And that is the right way."

Osho, *This very body the Buddha.*

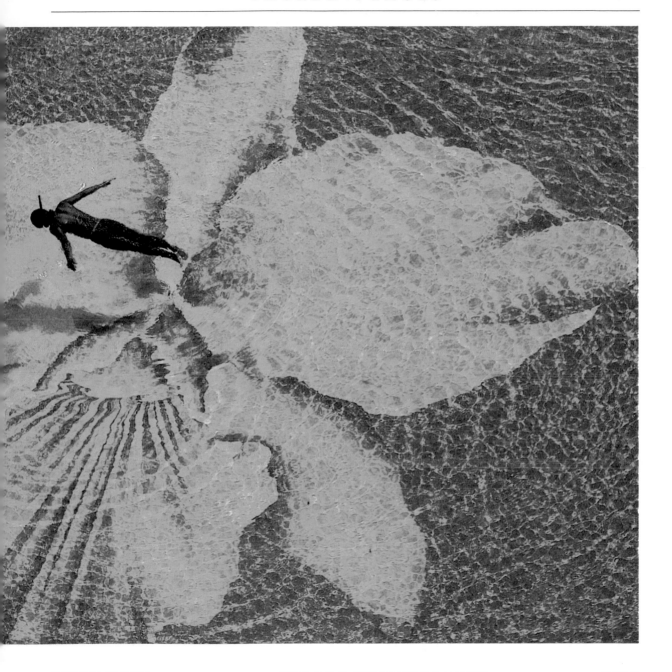

C H A P T E R   10

THE
ANCIENT MEASURERS

THE MAGIC ONE

A mongst all the modern assertions of scientific and technical understanding that have almost successfully drowned the magic of the ancients, there is the contrast between the old and new forms of measurement. In this century we blunder through schooling in a state of semi-lethargy and often complete boredom, under the influence of the cold hard "facts" of mathematics, believing, because no teacher has told us otherwise, that this is all there is to know. The "monument" of the examination that must, beyond all other religions, be worshiped so that we may continue into the adult religion of "earning", profoundly denies the actual power of understanding. For today's social indoctrination is stronger than any that has passed before, and there is little room in most people's lives for change away from this superficial "education".

Measurement, to the people of the ancient world, was not based on the concept of progress and the desire to succeed and increase, but on an overall understanding and love for the complete planet as a living creature within a living universe, whose health and prosperity was completely connected, indeed bound, to the people who lived within it. The lack of this connection today is, of course, the reason for the slow but inevitable destruction of our natural resources. The whole belief in numbers and measurement contained a structure and symbolism that placed it at the very beginning of man's connection with his nature around him. "Number" was number one! It was the first of

The Sphinx and the flying saucer. Some believe that these magnificent monuments from the distant passed are a reminder of the continued presence of flying machines from alien planets. Recent sightings in 1990 of unidentified flying objects, viewed by large numbers of people, indicate the possibility that these ideas may be justified.

Perhaps we are being watched by those who wait for us to get passed the chaos of our present age and into a more hospitable state so that they can come and meet us and be friendly. Perhaps then we will be introduced to greater sacredness outside our own world.

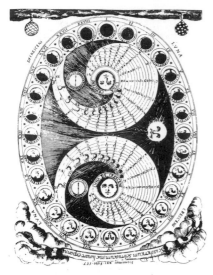

Above is a perpetual lunar calendar showing the phases of the moon. Kircher, the illustrator from the 17th century in Germany, designed the calendar to show the integrated nature of mathematics, mysticism and mythology. By using the natural growth properties of the spiral he has indicated that it is possible to read the hour of moonrise according to each successive phase. The two right-handed spirals, representing the waxing and waning moons, are mirror images of each other. Spirals are identified with the moon by relating the lunar phases to the solar phases or days. The spiral can also be related to the circle and thus to the male and female conditions.

firsts and laid down a pattern from which everything else moved.

To make this perhaps clearer to the modern mind – accustomed to thinking of numbers as merely part of the mathematical conditioning received from childhood – we can think of the basics of life. Go back to the very earliest thoughts. Life is laid out in a certain way – cyclic, patterned through always the same movements. The cycle of the moon is constant, moving through fixed and manifest numerical combinations. The patterns of music, arithmetic, astronomy, astrology, geometry, all contain the same numeric quality. The way we think in temporal movement, from past through present into future, contains the same numerical factors in the hours, minutes or days of our lives. We live always through the same proportions – height, weight, structure, belief and it appears also true that these numbers confirm the source and the result both at the same time, for they exist inside the human mind and outside it in the planet and universe it occupies. We think the same numbers as we see – naturally, for we are, after all inhabitants of the universe. But if we stop and consider this state of being it becomes strangely mystical, because it confirms to us that we are not separate from life but the same as life.

The ancient peoples of the world respected and venerated the study of numbers simply because within them lay the whole of human comprehension of movement. As we can understand that the same numerical system exists within music as it does within the measurement of the distance between earth and a star, or between the footsteps of a healthy human, so we can also see that these things exist harmoniously or discordantly within life, potentially, and that we, as humans, are eminently capable, especially during this century, of destroying that natural numeric harmony by losing the respect that we used to have for the numbers themselves.

For example, the essence of the number ONE, in the terms of the ancient beliefs, was that it represented the vital organism of the universe which operated as a whole, a single vibrating unit – a number ONE which was indivisible, unique, containing and generating all other numbers. When looked upon this way, the number one suddenly takes on rather vast significance! It ceases to be simply a figure on the page of an exercise book which evokes nothing more than boredom and progress towards the number two.

The science that lay behind this numerical significance was what we today would call "magic," insofar as it contained all manner of correspondences through natural principles, dynamics, equilibriums and coincidences which were totally reconciled through a solid and foundational belief in mankind as a derivation and container of the number ONE – the whole universe. The rules were different. Opposites were not thought of as different, but as an integral part of the same – you could not have love without hate, fear without excitement, life without death. The concept of the coincidence was simply understood by realizing that like things attract one another – what can be simpler than that, it's obvious enough!

This numerical awareness spread across all forms of appreciation of the divine. Stonehenge, for example, was built according to a precise numerical study. The mean diameter of the lintel ring of this ancient monument is 50.4 feet, one hundredth of one of the most famous of all numbers – 5040. The number 5040 is a "canonical" number, meaning that it contains more interpretations or factors than any other number, for its size. It is the product of the first seven numbers all multiplied together. It is divisible by every number up to ten. It was also the number of feet in the Greek mile.

This theme of fixed measurements being applied to ancient monuments has led many modern theorists to suggest that perhaps the temples of our oldest forefathers deliberately contained the encodification of their knowledge of the world.

In his book *The New View Over Atlantis*, John Michell takes a close and fascinating look at the encodification inherent in

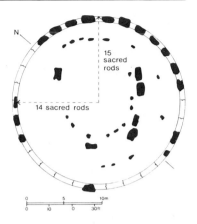

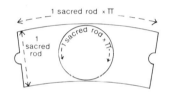

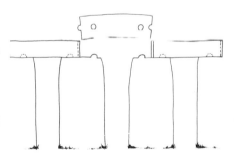

Stonehenge, as well as the extraordinary architectural skills that were employed to erect it, skills which we today would not be able to duplicate. The curved inner lintels form a circle, for example, that has a precise dimension equivalent to the Roman measure of a hundred feet. The width of the polished lintel stones gives an even more extraordinary reference according to Michell. The figure given for the width of the lintels themselves is 3.4757485 feet, a seemingly irrelevant decimal, until we compare it with the modern satellite surveys of the earth's polar radius – 20,854,491 feet – almost exactly six million times the Stonehenge lintel width! Dividing the polar radius by 200,000 we get the exact diameter of the outer lintel ring of Stonehenge, and the closer we look into the dimension of this unique monument the more we find that its measurements represent the dimensions of the Earth itself. And the system does not only apply to Stonehenge but also

The picture above depicts ancient "giants". These characters were believed to be the only ones who could possibly have been capable of carrying the stones needed to build stone circles such as Stonehenge. The vast weight of the stones could not possibly have been transported by ordinary mortals so that the ancients created mythology surrounding these huge giants as an answer to the problem.

to the ritual city of Teotihuacan in Mexico, and to the Jerusalem Temple, three extremely distant monuments with no apparent connection. How many more such monuments use the same measurements for their building? How did the people who built these sacred places know of such accurate measurement and how did they know the dimensions of the planet Earth when they are seen by us as essentially ignorant in relation to modern knowledge? And most extraordinary of all, how come they all used the same metrology? But the facts seem to define the truth. They *did* know the dimensions of the earth and they were easily sophisticated enough to encode them into complex measurement techniques.

As a small but apt observation in his wonderful book, Michell gives us some insight into the presence of the seemingly unlikely measurement of the "foot", so much denied now as a form, by the new acceptance of the meter.

"The distance round the equator, in which one degree contains the same number of feet as there are days in 1,000 years, reveals why it was that our foot (whose origins can be traced back to Sumerian metrology) provided the basic unit in the canon of earth measures. Unlike the other units in ancient metrology, which related to degrees of latitude and therefore had different values at different points round the earth, our foot unit measured a constant distance, a degree in the circle of the equator. It therefore had one value only, the same constant length which it has preserved to this day. How much more worthy of cultivation and study is this most venerable of human cultural possessions than the pretentious, mock-scientific metre! And yet how perfectly adapted is the metre, with its inherent banality and meaninglessness, to represent the values of the modern processes for which it was designed!"

To say that we have any clear idea about the ancient pagan religions and the motivations behind their extraordinary creations of monuments is false. We are only at the beginning of a vastly different and greatly exciting era of this planet's history when we will make discoveries that will shatter all of our standard beliefs in the sacred.

The meter is derived from the French meter, contrived in the 18th century and based on an inaccurate measurement of a quarter of the earth's circumference through the poles, of which the metre was supposed to be one ten-millionth part.

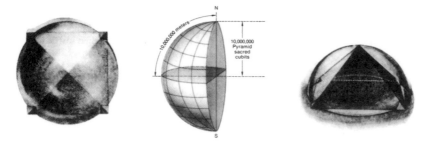

Measuring the Pyramid of Cheops

There is probably more fuss around the existence of the Pyramids than almost any other ancient monument on Earth. It satisfies a strong sense of the romantic in us and their particular shape has given rise, in recent years especially, to many esoteric beliefs including even the sharpening of razor blades. Books have been written providing some astonishing theories which tell us that, basically, either man could never have built the pyramids, especially that of Cheops, or if he did, it was the highest form of architecture ever to have been achieved on the planet during all of its history. And how can that be considering our advanced technology today? Why we should necessarily imagine that we have the highest skills available to us today, is a mystery to the writer of this book. We consider that the passing of time accords the increasing of wisdom – as though automatically. And yet in almost all other spheres of life, surrounded as we are by disaster, war, mass slaughter, pollution, imminent plague and ignorance, it is patently clear that we are far from the wisest of ages.

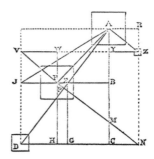

The Great Pyramid is certainly the most enigmatic of monuments where alone we must study the arts and crafts of the Egyptians for centuries more before we even begin to follow their logic and their understanding of life on Earth.

In every respect the Pyramid of Cheops seems to be a message from the past. Its four sides stand accurately to the four points of the compass, the orientation right on the line between the earth's two poles and at the apex of a quadrant of a circle containing the curve of the Nile Delta. It seems to stand as an ideally positioned marker for an earth survey. The most romantic of stories surrounding the construction of this glorious piece of architecture is that it is considered to be about four thousand years old, and according to biblical references, the age of the earth was 4,004 years at time of writing (the Bible, that is). As a result, there had hardly been enough time for the knowledge to build such a monument to have been accumulated – unless of course the knowledge was gained from divine sources. Thus, the building of the Pyramid of Cheops was attributed to the descendants of Noah himself. Much Christian Bible-thumping was derived from such intelligence!

In the detailed measuring of the Pyramid, it was discovered in fact to be an astonishing representation of both the planet on which it stands and the distances between the planets around it – not only the measurements of distance, but also of weight and shape of earth. Even more astonishing is that the chambers and vaults and passages inside the Pyramid of Cheops also record major historical events of the past and predictions of the future, one of which being that in the year 2,004 the present civilization of man will end! This, incidentally, concurs strangely with the prophecy of Nostradamus that 2,006 would see the greatest holocaust on Earth.

For anyone interested in the detailed measurements of the Pyramids, Michell's book, once again, is a remarkable reference, proving with great elegance that modern science has missed more than it has gained.

Perhaps the Pyramids are like light-houses for the entire planet – massive libraries of learning and secrets preserved for when mankind finally wakes up from the sleep that began when Christianity gave rise to the modern sciences.

The measurements of the Great Pyramid are like a secret story that unfolds before our very eyes, bringing the parts to a puzzle that may open up our knowledge of divinity beyond anything hereto conceived.
The same geometry has been around since the beginning of time and is employed today by the Masonic Lodges that still operate throughout America. Nothing is new that is not old.

Piazzi Smyth, in the illustration below demonstrated that the Great Pyramid's position in relation to the Nile Delta and the land surfaces of the globe gave an exact indication of the earth's axis and position in the cosmic movement.

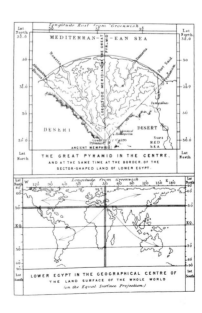

THE GREAT PYRAMID IN THE CENTRE, AND AT THE SAME TIME AT THE BORDER OF THE SECTOR-SHAPED LAND OF LOWER EGYPT.

LOWER EGYPT IN THE GEOGRAPHICAL CENTRE OF THE LAND SURFACE OF THE WHOLE WORLD (on the Equal Surface Projection.)

CHAPTER 11

THIS
SACRED PLACE

So Ancient,
So Foreign,

On this spread lies the magnificent Potala Palace at Llasa Tibet across the Kyichu River where the author spent some part of her youth. Here is an alien world, almost as strange as to be from another planet and as far away from the "reality" that most of us know as Mars itself.

We have spent the greater part of this book looking at ancient sacred traditions which date back so far in our history that it requires a great effort of imagination to suppose how life must have been for such people. It is almost as though they came from a different planet, and yet, there is something familiar, something that rings a bell within us, as though we still contain the essence of the beliefs they lived by.

If we take all the central features of the sacred places and peoples described herein – the Stone Age people, the Celts, the Hindus, Romans, Greeks, Egyptians, and the Christian Fathers – and look at the monuments that they created according to the old true faith, the pagan beliefs, those associated with Mother Earth and her intrinsic sacredness, we see almost as though through a clearing mist, a single effort, a response to life on Earth as part of life in the universe, of which man is as intrinsic as the grass and

So New

flowers, the trees and animals.

The building of the Pyramids is not necessarily attributed to Egyptian architects, the creation of Stonehenge is not certainly the work of those who were in exclusive occupation of the British Islands. We cannot be sure that any of the most significant monuments on Earth were necessarily of national character. Simply because our minds have become narrowed by bigoted attitudes does not necessarily mean that those minds of the past were the same. Life moved from one place to another – the Celts and Hindus originated from somewhere other than Europe and India, the English originated somewhere other than England. People hardly stood still in those days, for everything was fluctuating and developing. Our modern form of wisdom has little or nothing to do with that of the ancients and we cannot use our codes of behavior as yardsticks for their's.

Atlantis – the ultimate lost city, a place that may or may not exist as an example of all our hidden fantasies of the sacred. If we celebrate our planet at all, even in the slightest of our dreams, then all those dreams are as sacred as the solid monuments that fill the pages of this book. In any event they are for our delectation and hopefully will remain until all the human deficiencies are counteracting with love and understanding.

The evidence of the "international" nature of the builders of the great monuments seems to imply that there was some universal truth at work which did not derive its power from a fragmented attitude but from something global. As Michell states in his book *The new view over Atlantis:*

"The great riddle in the quest for the origin of human culture is that civilizations appear suddenly, at their peak, as if ready-made."

There are some, of course, who would imply that the knowledge was not merely global but cosmic, deriving from the visitations of other races who travelled from other planets in order to advance ours. But this idea, although quite reasonable and acceptable, is not strictly necessary as an explanation, for mankind possesses all that it needs in order to do all that he would alone, without help from outside.

The true conclusion lies more simply in areas where we accept the nature of life as a complete whole – a ONE – that is part of and wholly complete with the planet on which it resides. Simply because we do not today have the whole truth does not mean that others before us did not. Our avenue of interest, through the machinations of modern science and technology, may simply be the wrong avenue to truth. Perhaps the ancients of the past had it whereas we do not. Perhaps, indeed, the methods of the coming New Age of human potential will bring back a greater wisdom and refine our susceptibility to life enough to return the pagan religions and provide us with truth.

The official Vatican dogma, if we carefully examine its essence, derives from the understanding and fear of "popular religions," those belief structures that are today growing in strength, for popular religions will eventually cause the downfall of the established Church probably within ten years – and the re-birth of the pagan strength. And once we re-comprehend the old true faith, perhaps we will come back into contact with the earth HERSELF.

BIBLIOGRAPHY

The Origins of the Sacred – Anne Bancroft – Arkana
The Glory of the Holy Land – Shlomo S. Gafni/A. Van der Heyden – Steimatzky
The Book – Osho – Rebel Publishing.
The New View Over Atlantis – John Michell – Thames & Hudson
Atlantis – Charles Berlitz – Putnam
Secrets of the Ice Age – Evan Hadingham
The Power of Myth – Joseph Campbell – Doubleday
Zen, Pointing to Reality – Thames and Hudson.
Celtic Mysteries – Thames and Hudson
The Mystic Spiral – Thames and Hudson
The Secret Country – Janet and Colin Bord – Paladin
A Land of Gods and Giants – Mick Sharp – Alan Sutton
5/5/2000: Ice—The Ultimate Disaster – Richard W. Noone – Harmony
The Celts – T.G.E. Powell – Thames & Hudson
Unknown Man – Yatri – Simon & Schuster Inc.
Civilization Before Greece and Rome – H.W.F. Saggs – Batsford
Antico Oriente – André Parrot – Arnoldo Mondadori
Buckland's Complete Book of Witchcraft – Llewelyn
Book of the Hopi – Frank Waters – Penguin
Living Buddhism – Andrew Powell – British Museum
The Secret of the Golden Flower – Richard Wilhelm – Arkana
Sufi, Expressions of the Mystic Quest – Laleh Bekhtiar – Thames & Hudson
L'Arte Nella Storia Dell'Uomo – Giunti
Drawing Down the Moon – Margot Adler – Beacon Press
The Four Elements – Margaret Gullan-Whur – Century Hutchinson
Lourdes, City of the Virgin – Bonechi
Pompeii, 2000 Years Ago
The Mystic Life of Merlin – R.V. Stewart – Arkana
Points of Cosmic Energy – Blanche Merz – C.W. Daniel & Company Ltd.

ACKNOWLEDGMENTS

The author would like to thank the following for their help in making this book possible:
Everyone at Labyrinth Publishing, especially the Italian crew – Philip Dunn, Sandipa Gould Griffin
and the space in India – Merlin's madness and Manuela.
Also thanks to the following photographers and agencies for the kind use of their pictures in the book:
Labyrinth Picture Library – 3, 10, 12/13, 25, 26, 28, 29, 30, 34, 43, 56, 61, 83, 96/97, 99, 105, 106, 115, 131, 140/1, 146, 150, 169, 177, 187, 199, 200, 201.
National Aerophotography Service – Peru´– 9, 169
K.B. Kaplan USA – 23, 223
Robert Fludd – 38
Laughing Man Institute – 184
Krishnamurti Foundation – 184
Douglas Johnson – "Rio Grande" USA – 7
Rajneesh Foundation, Poona, India – 16, 18, 51, 190/191, 192/193, 194, 195, 196, 203
Roger Dean, Magnetic Storm – 219
Sandipa Gould Griffin, Labyrinth, Switzerland – 22, 55, 104, 178, 179
Crystal Art, Poona, India – 19, 54, 102
Women of the Celts, Inner Traditions International – 86
Gianluca De Santis, Calci, Italy – 42, 183
Tibetan Book of the Dead, Shambala Dragon Editions – 186
P. Chesley, Hawaii – 207
Seven Arrows – 143, 162, 164/5, 163, 166
Chicago Natural History Museum – 161
British Museum, Graham Harrison – 182, 220/1
Monastery of San Lorenzo, Italy – 171
Bruno Kortenhorst – 31, 39
Yatri, Florence – 197